ENOCH THE BLESSED SEER
BY
DAVID DOWSON

**Other books also written
by David Dowson include:**

Chess for Beginners
Chess for Beginners Edition 2
Into the Realm of Chess Calculation
Nursery Rhymes
The Path of a Chess Amateur
CHESS: the BEGINNER'S GUIDE eBook:

NOVELS
Declon Five
Dangers Within
The Murder of Inspector Hine
Spooks Scarlett's Enigma
The Deception Unveiled
Webs of Blood and Shadows
Night Assassin
Cloak of Deception
Being Mini Lakshmi

Contents

Chapter 1: The Blessing of Enoch 3

Chapter 2: Enoch In Search of the Lost Word 13

Chapter 3: The Vision of the Holy One 27

Chapter 4: The Day of Tribulation.............................36

Chapter 5: Enoch's Revelation 54

Chapter 6: The Angels' Message 64

Chapter 7: The Holy Great One.................................72

Chapter 8: The Coming Fear.....................................78

Chapter 9: The Quaking Watchers 87

Chapter 10: Trembling Ends.....................................99

Chapter 12: The Call of Enoch............................118

Chapter 14: Filled with Awe and Reverence..........142

Chapter 15: A Journey of Gratitude 159

Chapter 16: Embracing the Sacred Purpose 174

Chapter 18: A Gift of Connection............................205

Chapter 19: Walking the Chosen Path 225

Chapter 20: The Unfolding of Divine Visions 245

CHAPTER 1: THE BLESSING OF ENOCH

Jared moved with the exhaustion of a man crippled by the weariness of living through centuries as he knelt on the fertile earth. Unlike him, the world was younger, colourful, and teeming with lifestyles after the expulsion from Eden. A hollowness gnawed at him, and despite his consistently righteous ways, his spouse, Barthena, remained barren. Their prayers for a child seemed to go unanswered. A heavenly traveller bathed their humble abode one luminous night in an otherworldly peace. An angel, radiant as 1000 suns, descended and spoke in a voice that vibrated through Jared's bones, "Barthena shall conceive a toddler not like any other. He will walk hand in hand with the divine, a bridge between heaven and earth." Barthena's pregnancy became not like another. The air crackled with unseen electricity around her, plant life bloomed out of season anyplace she stepped, and heavenly music seemed to follow her every move. When

Enoch emerged, he wasn't a wailing babe but a cooing child with eyes that shimmered with a sense of inner peace. Even as a little one, Enoch's extreme good became evident. He spoke in entire sentences before his first year, his phrases sporting an awareness beyond his age. Animals, normally wary of humans, flocked to him, nuzzling his fingers and following him anywhere. Plants thrived below his contact, leaves unfurling and flora blooming quicker in his presence. One starlit night, as Jared gazed upon the marvel that became his son, Enoch grew to become his luminous eyes upwards. He began to talk in the language of shimmering constellations. Jared, eyes wide with awe, diagnosed the constellations his ancestors had spoken of but arranged in a manner he'd never seen before. They shaped a map, a pathway leading beyond the heavens. News of Enoch's gifts unfolds a long way and is vast. People journeyed from remote lands to witness the child who spoke with the stars. He calmed raging beasts with a touch, healed the ill with a phrase, and brought forth rain all through droughts with an easy prayer. Yet, no matter the awe he inspired, Enoch remained humble. He played with different youngsters, helped his parents with chores, and stated the divine with the same innocence as he observed the clouds. Enoch's start, a beacon of hope in a world developing ever more remote from God, marked him as a being unlike every other. He was a testimony to the divine, a bridge between the human and the heavenly, a harbinger of a destiny wherein religion and surprise walked hand in hand. Enoch, now a younger guy with the electricity of a pro-farmer and the grace of a wasteland gazelle, changed into an acquainted sight at some stage in the bustling village. His days were riddled with many interactions, reflecting his ability to connect to anybody. For the weary elders accrued inside the colour of the ancient banyan tree, Enoch changed into an affected person listener. He might sit beside them, eyes reflecting the knowledge etched on their faces as they told tales of the beyond and issues concerning destiny. He did not offer empty platitudes but quiet information that soothed their anxieties. His touch, light as a feather, on their gnarled arms sometimes eased aches higher than any poultice. For the boisterous children chasing each other across the dusty streets, Enoch became a playful partner. He could outrun the swiftest with a speed that pierced through the air, and his testimonies, woven with fantastic creatures and heavenly trips, held them spellbound. He'd join their video games, transforming sticks into shimmering swords and pebbles into glowing orbs, their innocent imaginations fuelled by his touch. For the ostracised widow struggling to hold her meagre farm, Enoch becomes a tireless helper. He'd mend fences with an energy that belied his lean body, coax wilting plants again to life with a whispered prayer, and proportion his harvest to ensure her pantry remained full. He spoke to her of chores, the sundown's beauty, the human spirit's resilience, and the divine's unwavering love.

Even the surliest blacksmith, regarded for his gruff demeanour and even gruff mood, found himself softening in Enoch's presence. Enoch wouldn't interfere with his hammering, but now and then, at the same time as the forge roared, he'd start to hum a wordless melody. The reputedly random notes would weave themselves into the rhythmic clanging of the hammer on steel, developing a strangely beautiful symphony. The blacksmith would initially greet him with resistance, only to find his anger dissipating, shrouded by a sense of sudden peace. Enoch didn't preach or demand reverence. He lived his actions with a consistent sermon on kindness, compassion, and a deep connection with the divine. His presence, a bridge no longer simply among heaven and earth but among the hearts of his community, fostered an experience of solidarity and belonging that has been waning in the younger world. The afternoon sun beat down on the village, baking the clay houses and turning the dusty streets into shimmering mirages. A younger girl, playing with a discarded flint close to a pile of dry leaves, did not understand that the spark that danced upwards might morph into a hungry beast. By the time she shrieked, flames had been licking on the thatched roof of her family's home. Panic erupted like a wildfire itself. Mothers clutched youngsters, guys scrambled for buckets, their shouts a determined refrain towards the growing roar of the inferno. Flames fuelled through the dry summertime air began to crawl across the roof, threatening to leap to neighbouring houses. Coming back from a solitary stroll in the hills, Enoch saw the smoke billowing from afar. A surge of urgency propelled him forward. He burst into the village square simply as the fire erupted fully, casting an ominous glow on the panicked faces. Without hesitation, Enoch waded into the chaos. His voice was calm amidst the rising hysteria as it rose above the noise. He directed the guys to properly form a human chain from the village to the burning house. Women have been advised to moist clothes and bedsheets, creating a makeshift barrier between the flames and the encompassing houses. However, the well water was not sufficient. Fanned by an unexpected gust of wind, the flames threatened to engulf the complete shape. In that important second, Enoch did something awesome. He raised his palms toward the sky, eyes closed in concentration. A hush fell over the crowd. A shift within the wind becomes the primary sign. Instead of feeding the flames, it started to push them again, far from the neighbouring houses. Then it was raining. Not a heavy downpour but a gentle, persistent drizzle that seemed to appear out of nowhere. It soaked the burning thatch, dampening its fury. Enoch diminished his palms, a faint smile playing on his lips. As the rain intensified, extinguishing the flames absolutely, cheers erupted from the crowd. Tears of comfort streamed down their faces, replaced by smiles of gratitude as they embraced one another. No one became harmed. The fire had been contained to the unmarried residence, leaving the back of a smouldering shell but no casualties. As the villagers surveyed the damage, they looked at Enoch with a newfound reverence. He was not just a man of kindness and compassion; he became a bridge among them and the divine, a residing testimony to the energy of religion and the dazzling. Later that night, as the village amassed underneath the starlit sky, sharing tales and rebuilding their sense of community, Enoch sat quietly beside his mother and father. He knew his moves were now not his doing but a present from a better power. He had been a vessel, a conduit for the divine intervention that saved their homes and lives. And as he looked at the grateful faces around him, a warm temperature bloomed in his chest – a sense of belonging and reason- that solidified his vicinity as a beacon of hope on this young and ever-evolving globe. Enoch's vibrant and unsettling goals reminded him of his specific connection to the divine. They hinted at a future wherein his reason lay – to be a bridge between humanity and the heavenly realm, to apply his presence to guide his humans closer to a course of righteousness and guard them against the darkness that loomed on the horizon. Even as a toddler, Enoch's desires contrasted with any other. One night, a vibrant scene unfolded earlier than him. The sky, commonly a comforting expanse of twinkling stars, fractured open like a shattered mirror. Through the jagged tear, a stunning sight appeared, revealing a heavenly city built on clouds. Majestic beings with wings of heart moved through the streets, their voices resonating like thunderous hymns. Fear gripped younger Enoch, but a feeling of awe overshadowed it. He woke with a puff, the photograph of the heavenly city seared into his memory, a regular reminder of an international past of his personal life. These desires fuelled Enoch's movements. He interacted with his community not simply out of kindness but with a deep-seated choice to foster unity and knowledge – a reflection of the heavenly harmony he had seen in his dreams. As Enoch grew older, his desires became more complex and prophetic. In one, he decided his status on a barren, desolate tract. The once fertile floor became cracked and patched, and the vibrant existence of his village was changed by skeletal timber and lifeless rivers. The air hung heavy with melancholy, and a low, mournful cry seemed to emanate from the very earth itself. An ancient and sorrowful voice echoed in his mind, "Have you forgotten me, child of light? My bounty withers, my creatures perish, all because of man's folly." Enoch awoke with a heavy heart, the dream a stark caution of a future he desperately hoped to prevent. His interactions with the community took on a new urgency. He became a champion for the environment, teaching sustainable practices and urging recognition for the delicate balance of nature. He knew that the future he dreamt of, the heavenly metropolis bathed in concord, could not exist on a ravaged planet. Another ordinary dream featured a giant, swirling sea of stars. Unlike the acquainted constellations, those were ever-moving, forming styles and emblems that pulsed with an otherworldly light. As

Enoch focused, the symbols coalesced, revealing themselves as a language. This historic script held the universe's secrets. A gentle and effective voice whispered in his ear, "Learn, child, for information is the bridge between worlds. Use it to guide your humans, to heal the rifts among heaven and earth."

CHAPTER 2: ENOCH IN SEARCH OF THE LOST WORD

Laughter echoed throughout the half-empty streets as Enoch raced his friends, a basket bouncing rhythmically at his hip. Maya, her darkish braids whipping in the back of her, shrieked in pride as she chased him, a mischievous glint in her hazel eyes. Bringing up the rear, lumbered Ben, a massive boy with a perpetual grin and a loaf of bread precariously balanced on his head. Completing their group was Sarah, her brown curls escaping the confines of a woven headband, humming a music tune that spoke of her contentment as she ran a hand through a group of wildflowers. The concept for the picnic had sprung from a lazy afternoon spent underneath the village banyan tree. The noon solar had forged dappled shadows on their faces as they shared tales, each more fantastical than the final. Enoch, stimulated by a dream of a shimmering meadow bathed in sunlight, had proposed a breakout from the village walls.

"Let's mission past the barley fields," he had cautioned, his voice filled with an adventurous spirit. "There's a hidden valley whispered in tales that now only exist in the elders' memories, a place of wildflowers and babbling brooks." The idea sparked instantaneous pleasure. Maya, ever the explorer, bounced with enthusiasm. Ben, who found joy in something concerning meals, effortlessly agreed, envisioning a picnic spread suited for a king. Even Sarah, typically content with her quiet observations, could not resist the attraction of a mister heaven. The following couple of days had been a whirlwind of guidance.

Maya and her nimble arms wove a beautiful picnic blanket from reeds and wildflowers. Under Enoch's watchful eye, Ben baked a batch of honeyed buns that promised to soften their mouths. Sarah and her keen eye for herbs assembled a clean pitcher of lemongrass tea. Enoch continually consulted a historic scroll, decoding cryptic guidelines that caused the hidden valley. Finally, the day arrived. The air crackled with anticipation as they converged at the village gate. With baskets overflowing with their arrangements and hearts brimming with excitement, they prompt, their laughter over excited through a light breeze. The hidden valley became a breathtaking sight when they eventually discovered it.

Lush meadows carpeted the floor, dotted with colourful blooms that hummed with unseen bugs. A clear flow snaked along the valley floor, its surface shimmering like polished silver. Sunlight dappled through the leaves of towering bushes, growing a mosaic of light and shadow on the ground. They spread their blanket beneath an incredibly majestic oak, its branches heavy with ripening acorns. Laughter erupted as Ben, after a playful tussle with Maya, ended up sprawled on the blanket, his valuable bread miraculously intact. Sccaptivated by a flitting butterfly, Sarah wove a crown of wildflowers, placing it gently on Maya's head, who giggled, her dark eyes glowing with satisfaction. As they feasted on their picnic spread, sharing testimonies and dreams below the watchful gaze of the ancient oak, an experience of perfect contentment settled over them. In this hidden paradise, they have been not simply friends but a family, certain by shared laughter and a love for the wonders surrounding them. In this moment, time is regarded to face, nevertheless. The worries of the village, the whispers of a future yet to unfold, all diminished away, replaced with the aid of the easy pleasure of friendship and the beauty of their secret haven.

Sated on honeyed buns and lemongrass tea, their laughter echoing through the hidden valley, Enoch felt an acquainted pull. This time, it was not hunger or a thirst for adventure but a deeper, more subtle beckoning. Excusing himself from his friends, he saw a barely discernible direction that meandered far from the clearing. The path led him deeper into the valley's heart, where daylight struggled to penetrate the dense canopy of historic bushes. The air grew cooler, a welcome respite from the afternoon sun. Pushing apart a curtain of vines, Enoch stumbled upon a sight that sent a jolt through him. Carved into the facet of a towering cliff, the face became a hidden cave. Its front, partly obscured by moss and ferns, seemed to exude an air of forgotten secrets and techniques. Curiosity warring with a sliver of apprehension, Enoch stepped in. The cave became cool and damp, with waves of mist filtering through cracks in the rock's surface. Yet, as his eyes adjusted, a breathtaking scene spread out. The cavern was not simply a hollow area. It became a meticulously crafted repository, its partitions coated with ornately carved shelves. A stunning series of artefacts rested on them – polished stones etched with intricate symbols, clay tablets inscribed with an unknown language, and scrolls of age-worn leather that breathed ancient records. Enoch was attracted to a particular shelf and saw a book unlike any he had ever seen. Its cover, made from a shimmering, iridescent stone, pulsed with an inner light. Hesitantly, he opened it, revealing pages full of symbols that danced earlier than his eyes. Though the language was foreign, a single word appeared to leap off the web page, burning itself into his memory: "HaShem Asher Bachar" – a melody without music, a promise shrouded in mystery. A shiver ran down his backbone, a bizarre experience of familiarity washing over him. He did not understand the phrases, yet they resonated within him, wearing the weight of forgotten understanding and reality yet to be found out. Returning to the picnic site, Enoch found his friends sprawled contentedly inside the shade, their faces flushed with laughter and their bellies full. He joined them, a piece of the hidden cave and its secrets tucked away in his heart. The phrase, "HaShem Asher Bachar," echoed in his mind, a steady reminder of the splendid discovery and the unanswered questions it brought. As the day wore on, the reminiscence of the picnic dwindled right into a loved memory, replaced by the burning member of the inscription. Enoch knew, with a certainty that defied logic, that this discovery held the key to something profound – a part of his reason, a whisper from the divine echoing through the ages. The inscription, a melody without a tune, might grow to be the guiding big name on his adventure, leading him toward a destiny yet to be completely understood. Enoch keeps dreaming of the word from the cave and tries to derive it by journeying to the metropolis library. The idyllic memory of the picnic within the hidden valley becomes slowly eclipsed by using an extra pressing problem – the cryptic phrase, "HaShem Asher Bachar," that Enoch had met inside the ancient cave. It haunted his goals, a melody without a tune that rang through his mind, traumatising his thoughts. Sleep added no solace, best-fragmented visions of swirling symbols and the weight of an unknown truth. Driven by an insatiable interest and a nascent sense of purpose, Enoch is determined to try to find solutions. The village elder, a repository of forgotten lore, offered no insights into the atypical inscription. Disappointment gnawed at Enoch, but it simply fueled his remedy. The answer, he realised, would not be figured out in whispered folktales but in an extra scholarly pursuit. The following nights were a tale of moments filled with desires. Enoch saw himself again within the cool, cavernous embodiment of the hidden cave, the inscription "HaShem Asher Bachar ' pulsating at the historic ebook like a living ember. The abnormal symbols appeared to writhe and shift, beckoning him nearer, promising a revelation beyond his grasp. He would wake with a start, the word echoing in his thoughts, a melody without a song that resonated with an otherworldly energy. Inscription has become an obsession. It shadowed his every waking concept, a continual itch he could not scratch. Sharing it with his friends was not an option. The revel within the cave held a sacred great, a secret entrusted to him alone. He wanted answers, and with a growing experience of urgency, he decided to look for them within the one area that housed the knowledge of their village – the library. The library became a modest structure, its walls coated with scrolls and clay drugs meticulously labelled. With a continually worried frown and spectacles perched precariously on his nostril, the vintage librarian greeted Enoch with a curt nod. Enoch, heart pounding in his chest, explained his dilemma. He defined the cave, the inscription, and the haunting melody of the unknown language. The librarian listened patiently, his brow furrowing further with every phrase. When Enoch finished, a heavy silence descended upon the room. Finally, the librarian spoke, his voice a dry rasp. "The language you describe," he gasped, "is an archaic dialect spoken before the outstanding flood. Few texts remain, and the ones that do are incomplete, their meanings shrouded in obscurity." Disappointment washed over Enoch. He had come looking for solutions but only ran into a dead end. The inscription, it seemed, became a relic of a forgotten age, a whisper lost to the sands of time. Dejected, he thanked the librarian and left the confines of the library, the load of the unknown urgent down on him. Back in his room, under the watchful gaze of the moon, Enoch stared at the ceiling. Although he did not understand the inscription, he felt it was sizable. It became a bit of a puzzle, a shard of a mirror reflecting a truth he desperately craved. He knew then that his quest for which means had best begun. The library may not have held the answers. Still, it had ignited a fire within him, a determination to resolve the secrets and techniques of the inscription, regardless of the price. Enoch stood upon the holy mountain, his heart filled with awe and reverence for the super Creator of all. The sun shone down upon him, its warm temperature a comforting embrace, as he lifted his eyes to the heavens. At that moment, a voice spoke to him, a voice full of incandescence and beauty. "Enoch, blessed are you among mortals, selected to receive the sacred visions of the Highest," the voice whispered, sending shivers down Enoch's spine. Trembling with each fear and surprise, Enoch fell to his knees, tears streaming down his face as he felt the presence of divinity surrounding him. He knew he had been selected for a high-quality and holy motive that could forever change his life. Filled with an experience of humility and gratitude, Enoch raised his fingers to the sky and supplied a prayer of thanksgiving. He knew that his adventure had just started and would need all the power and courage he may want to muster to fulfil the future that lay before him. Enoch felt the weight of responsibility weigh heavily on his shoulders, which he knew he needed to carry with honour and integrity. The sacred visions he had come to obtain might no longer be intended to form just his course but also the fate of all humankind. As he gazed into the infinite expanse of the heavens, Enoch felt an experience of purpose and clarity wash over him. He knew that his connection to the divine became a present, one that he must cherish and nurture and that would allow him to fulfil his calling. With unwavering determination, Enoch rose from his knees. He set forth at the Most High's route, his spirit aflame with faith and braveness. The wind whispered words of encouragement as he walked, guiding his steps and putting forward his chosen future. And so, with a heart full of hope and faith, Enoch embarked on the journey of a lifetime, knowing that the divine presence could be his steady accomplice, guiding him through the rigours and tribulations ahead. The clouds above shifted and swirled, a dance of dew and shadow playing out throughout the sky. Enoch felt the heavens had been shaping up to reveal secrets and techniques lengthily saved and hidden from mortal eyes. The weight of the visions to come back pressed upon his thoughts, a reminder of the significance of the venture in advance. As he walked, Enoch felt an experience of a connection to the arena around him in contrast to something he had never known before. The earth below his feet felt alive, pulsing with unseen power and historical awareness. Every gust of wind carried a message, a whisper from the divine guiding him on his path. The stars above twinkled with a brilliance that seemed to speak of mysteries past mortal ability. Enoch's heart swelled with surprise and gratitude, knowing he was selected to see the divine plan unfold. With every step he took, Enoch felt the presence of the Most High developing more potent within him, filling him with an experience of purpose and clarity. He knew that the road in advance might be arduous and fraught with challenges, but he also knew that he would not be by himself. The hand of the Almighty might guide him, and the light of fact might illuminate his way. And so, with his heart filled with faith and his spirit ablaze with dedication, Enoch continued his adventure to get hold of the sacred visions that might shape humankind's destiny for generations to come back.

CHAPTER 3: THE VISION OF THE HOLY ONE

The village, though small, boasted a modest library – a set of scrolls and drugs meticulously kept by a wizened pupil named Ezra. Enoch approached him with a combination of trepidation and wish, his heart pounding as he described the hidden cave and the inscription that burned itself into his reminiscence. Ezra, his bushy eyebrows knitting collectively in awareness, listened carefully. When Enoch finished, a flicker of recognition sparked in the antique guy's eyes. He shuffled away to a dusty corner of the library, returning with a scroll some distance older than Enoch had ever seen. The parchment, brittle and fragile, became inscribed with a language that closely resembled the symbols from the cave. "This," Ezra rasped, his voice burdened with years, "is an archaic shape of textual content, a language spoken in a time before our ancestors even settled those lands." Hope surged through Enoch. Here, possibly, lay the key to unlocking the mystery. With patience born of years spent interpreting historic texts, Ezra launched into a slow and laborious translation. Days became weeks as they wrestled with the cryptic language, each new revelation leading to more questions. Finally, a breakthrough arrived. Pointing to a selected segment of the translated textual content, Ezra's voice trembled with awe, "Here it's far, Enoch. 'HaShem Asher Bachar' — it interprets to 'The Name That Was Chosen.'" Enoch's breath hitched. The Name That Was Chosen? What name may want to keep such electricity, such importance? Ezra, his very own eyes huge with marvel, persisted, "This text speaks of a being, a divine entity distinguished by this chosen name. It speaks of a covenant, a promise made among this entity and humanity." The revelation sent shivers down Enoch's spine. The inscription within the cave, a melody without a tune, changed into a fraction of a forgotten covenant, a whisper of a promise made among the divine and humankind. The weight of this information settled on him, a responsibility he did not fully apprehend but one he innately knew he had a function to play in. Leaving the library, Enoch walked with a newfound cause. The inscription became now not just a haunting word but a key, a fraction of a heavenly map, leading him toward a future far grander than he ought to have ever imagined. The dream of the heavenly town and the warnings of a desolate destiny seemed to converge in this revelation of the significance of the Name That Was Chosen. Enoch knew his journey had come a long way from over. He had a fact to uncover, a covenant to understand. But with every step and a new piece of ability he gleaned, he felt a growing fact – he became on the path he was supposed to stroll, the bridge between humanity and the divine. The dream opened with a readability that left Enoch breathless. He saw himself standing on a mountaintop bathed in an airy light. The air vibrated with an unseen energy, and a feeling of awe so profound it bordered on terror gripped him. Then, a huge and powerful voice resonated through his very being. "Enoch," the voice boomed, shaking the very foundations of the mountain. "You stand at the precipice of understanding." Enoch, trembling, controlled an unmarried word, "Who...?" "I am the Holy One," the voice resonated, "the supply of all that is, the light that pierces the darkness." Enoch bowed his head and was conquered by his presence. He felt small, insignificant, a trifling speck against the vastness of the divine. "You have been selected," the voice persevered, "now not because you are the most powerful or the wisest, but due to the fact you possess a heart that yearns for knowledge, a bridge among humanity and the heavens." Enoch dared to elevate his eyes. He saw not a stunning light but a discern cloaked in swirling mist, its functions obscured yet by some means reassuring. "The inscription that problems you," the voice persevered, "is a fragment of a forgotten prophecy. It speaks of 'HaShem Asher Bachar' - The One Who Chooses. It is a promise, Enoch, of a destiny where humanity and the divine walk hand in hand." Enoch's heart pounded. "But why me? I am just a simple guy." "Because, Enoch," the voice softened, a touch of tenderness seeping into its vastness, "you carry within you the capability for both superb compassion and unwavering religion. You see the sector not just with your eyes but together with your heart. You are the bridge, the only one who can guide your people toward a destiny bathed in righteousness." Enoch felt a surge of heat spread through him. The inscription, desires, and bizarre pull toward the divine started making sense. He was not only a guy with strange gifts but a vessel chosen to bring in a brand-new generation. "But the path will not be easy," the voice continued, be aware of warning creeping in. "Darkness will rise in search of severing the relationship between heaven and earth. You will face trials, doubt, and despair." Fear snaked through Enoch, chilling him despite the warm celestial temperature surrounding him. "Yet, you may no longer be alone," the voice reassured him. "I may be with you, a guiding light in the darkest nights. Remember, Enoch, your cause is not simply to apprehend but to bridge the gap, to lead your people toward the light." The dream began to vanish, the mountaintop dissolving into swirls of light. Enoch woke with a gasp, the phrases of the Holy One echoing in his mind. A newfound resolve settled in his chest. He changed into selected, no longer for his glory but for a more distant purpose. The inscription, a promise veiled in a thriller, now held a deeper meaning. It was not only a message from the beyond but a map for destiny, a destiny he, Enoch, could help construct. The weight of his duty was heavy, but alongside it bloomed a feeling of reason, a burning preference to satisfy his future because of the bridge between humanity and the divine. As the Holy One continued to talk, his words resonated with an undying wisdom that transcended the restrictions of mortal information. He delved deeper into the mysteries of introduction, unveiling the problematic internet of interconnectedness that bound all residing beings together in an unbroken sequence of life. He saw the unseen forces that guided the ebb and flow of the universe, of ways the cosmic energies interplayed to weave the fabric of fact itself. He revealed the subtle nuances of the soul's adventure, of how each lifestyle became a thread in the grand design of cosmic evolution, contributing to the unfolding of awareness. The villagers listened with rapt interest, their hearts increasing with each revelation. They felt a profound experience of awe and marvel at the vastness of the cosmos and their infinitesimal location within it. The Holy One's phrases sparked an interest inside them, urging them to discover the depths of their being and the divine spark that lay dormant within them. As night descends night descended on the village, casting a blanket of darkness over the land, the Holy One's voice carried on the gentle night breeze, weaving a spell of appeal that enraptured all who listened with an otherworldly glow, their light illuminating the course of souls in search of truth and enlightenment. And so, as the night wore on and the villagers of Enoch remained enthralled by the Holy One's teachings, a profound transformation happened inside their hearts and minds. They felt harmony with all the introductions, a deep connection to the everlasting rhythm of the universe that pulsed inside their beings. In that sacred moment, the boundaries of the self dissolved, and a transcendent peace washed over the village, suffusing their souls with a profound feeling of oneness and concord. The Holy One's presence lingered within the air like a benediction, a reminder that they have been now not by me in their journey toward enlightenment but had been guided and supported by unseen forces of affection and light. And so, because the first light of dawn started to interrupt over the horizon, the villagers of Enoch stirred from their reverie, carrying with them the awareness and beauty of the Holy One's teachings deep within their hearts. Ready to face the demanding situations and benefits that awaited those days, they progressed into the new day with courage and religion, understanding that they were forever linked to the eternal dance of creation.

CHAPTER 4: THE DAY OF TRIBULATION

The dream descended upon Enoch with the burden of a shroud. One moment, he became nestled in his acquainted mattress, the gentle snores of his mother and father a comforting historical past hum. Then, he stood on a rise overlooking the fields that sustained his village. But the scene that greeted him was not the verdant beauty he knew. It became a wasteland. Once vibrant and inexperienced, the land was now a canvas of parched brown. The sun beat down mercilessly, baking the cracked earth into a desolate expanse. Skeletal stalks of corn, their husks empty and leaves dry and brittle, rattled in a warm, dry wind that carried no promise of rain. Once heavy with life-giving bounty, fruit trees stood like gaunt sentinels, their branches devoid of blossoms or even the whisper of leaves. A deathly silence hung heavy inside the air, as damaging as the rasping cries of crows circling overhead. Their harsh caws echoed within the emptiness, adding a layer of melancholy to the already desolate scene. Enoch felt a cold dread pool in his belly as he walked through this panorama. He came upon an old farmer, his face etched with the deep lines of an existence spent running the land. But these were not the strains of enjoyment or pleasure; they were etched with despair. The farmer clutched a handful of dusty earth in his calloused arms, the soil crumbling through his palms like dry sand. As Enoch approached, the farmer looked up, his eyes reflecting a horrible knowledge that sent chills down Enoch's backbone. "The land is loss of life," the farmer croaked, his voice raspy from disuse. "The blessing is long gone." His words resonated with a profound truth, a feeling of loss so deep that it reverberated in Enoch's very being. This was not only a barren panorama; it became a dwelling testament to a broken connection, a severed bond between the land and the divine. Enoch desperately desired to ask for evidence to understand how this may have occurred. But the farmer stared at the dead earth, his shoulders slumped in defeat. In that second, Enoch noticed a mirrored image of his fear, a glimpse of the destiny his village confronted if this blight took root. He woke with a pant, sweat clinging to his skin like a shroud. The dream lingered, a vivid memory etched into his thoughts. It was not just the desolate panorama that haunted him but the farmer's resigned attractiveness, the feeling of helplessness inside the face of this enormous and horrible loss. The inscription, "HaShem Asher Bachar" – The One Who Chooses – echoed his thoughts with a brand-new urgency. The choice was not a destiny filled with light but about keeping off the darkness that threatened to engulf his home. Once a supply of existence and sustenance, the land was now a symbol of a damaged covenant. It became a stark reminder of their energy dependence more than themselves. This electricity had grown to become its return on them. A feeling of responsibility settled upon Enoch's shoulders. The dream was a warning call, a glimpse into a future he could not allow. He did not apprehend the inscription yet, but he knew it held the key to restoring the balance, to rekindling the connection between the land and the divine. He needed to find a way to assuage the One Who Chooses through prayer, interpretation of historical texts, or anything vital. The reminiscence of the barren fields, the farmer's hopelessness, and the chilling wind carrying the echoes of crows might all be a stark reminder of the results of inactivity. The dream was not just a nightmare; it changed into a prophecy, a name to arms. Enoch, chosen with the aid of the divine, would not allow his village to descend into desolation. He would bridge the distance, find the solution, and produce lifestyles again to the land earlier than it became too overdue. Enoch jolted wide awake, gasping for air. His heart hammered against his ribs like a frantic chook trapped in a cage. The dream, a chilling tableau of destruction, clung to him like cobwebs, refusing to be brushed away. He found himself bathed in moonlight, its silvery luminescence a stark assessment of the horrors he had seen. The imaginative and prescient replayed in his mind, vibrant and frightening. The rectangular village, a hub of interest, lay deserted in his dreamscape. An unnatural wind, a fierce beast shorn of all mercy, lashed on the empty streets. Dust whipped right into a swirling dervish, obscuring the whole lot in its course. But it was not the wind that dispatched a shiver down Enoch's backbone, but the sound it carried – a howling symphony of terror. The howls originated from gigantic creatures that materialised from the dirt typhoon. Their paperwork, a gruesome amalgamation of nightmare and truth, was unlike whatever Enoch had ever seen. Twisted limbs, honed to ripping flesh, replaced arms. Their faces, if faces they can be known as, bore a scary resemblance to human visages, contorted into perpetual snarls of hunger. Glowing embers, devoid of heat, burned in their sockets, illuminating the route of destruction they carved through the village. The creatures attacked with a ferocity born of natural malice. Their claws, tipped with darkness that regarded light itself, ripped through the wooden walls of houses with sickening ease. Enoch noticed villagers, faces etched with terror, screaming for help. But their cries had been quickly silenced, misplaced in the cacophony of the wind and the guttural howls of the creatures. He watched, helpless, as his beloved village, a place of laughter and network, became reduced to a battlefield. The familiar warmth of his domestic, the heady scent of his mom's baking bread, and the cadence of his father's storytelling all evaporated in the face of this large onslaught. A surge of protectiveness, primal and fierce, roared to life within Enoch. These were not simply villagers; they had been his human beings — his friends, his own family. Fear but became a fleeting traveller. It was quickly replaced by a burning determination to stop the carnage, to shield his cherished ones from the horrors he had seen. But how? The creatures appeared unstoppable, their darkness a tangible force that threatened to engulf the whole lot in its path. Enoch's hands clenched into fists, nails digging into his fingers. He became just one guy, an easy villager with dreams now regarded more like childish fantasies. Yet, the faint yet insistent voice whispered from inside – the voice of the Holy One from a preceding dream. "You are selected," it had echoed, "a bridge between humanity and the heavens." Hope, a fragile ember, flickered to lifestyles in despair. He thought that desires were not only a caution but a manual. The inscription he carried within him, "HaShem Asher Bachar " – The One Who Chooses – held the key to saving his people. A surge of urgency pushed him from his bed. He could not stay paralyzed by fear. He had to act, to find a way to apply his presents, his connection to the divine, to combat the darkness he had seen. The moon held an eerie glow as Enoch stepped outside. Nevertheless, the air was silent and held not one of the fierce furies of his dream. Yet, he could not shake the sensation of being watched, of unseen eyes gazing at his every circulation. He appeared upon the celebrity-dusted canvas above, looking for a sign, a whisper of steering. The inscription echoed in his mind, a mantra towards the encroaching darkness. He did not have all the solutions, but he knew one issue: he would not let his goals become his village's reality. Dawn becomes approaching, portraying the eastern horizon with streaks of gold and red. With a newfound solution, Enoch set about preparing himself for the battle that changed into coming back. He might decipher the inscription, unencumbered by the secrets and techniques it held, and stand as a shield towards the darkness, a bridge between humanity and the divine, a protector of his human beings' destiny. The world dissolved into darkness. Enoch stood beside the acquainted well for one second, the heady scent of solar-baked earth and cool stone filling his nostrils. The next, the acquainted sounds of the village – the rhythmic hammering of the blacksmith, the playful shrieks of children – vanished, replaced by an oppressive silence. He changed into a loneliness, bathed in an unnatural gloom that appeared to emanate from the property itself. Enoch stumbled again, a chilly dread slithering down his spine. The niche, a source of lifeblood for generations, had turned out to be a gaping maw, its round rim no longer an image of sustenance but a gateway to something sinister. He peered down, his breath catching in his throat. The water, once a shimmering mirrored image of the sky above, became no more. A thick, oily blackness churned and roiled in its place, an unnatural luminescence emanating from its depths. The blackness was not, without a doubt, a shade; it felt sentient, alive with an evil intelligence. It writhed and pulsed, forming gruesome shapes that twisted and reformed with unsettling fluidity. Faces, some vaguely human, others huge and impossible, contorted in silent screams, their expressions a chilling reflection of his personal developing terror. A voice, a rasping whisper that echoed inside the significant emptiness of the nice, pierced through the oppressive silence. It changed into a voice devoid of warmth that scraped towards the very material of truth. "Your religion is weak," it hissed, the phrases slithering into his ears like venomous snakes. "Your connection to the divine is fading. Soon, darkness will devour it all." Enoch recoiled, the sheer malice dripping from the voice leaving him trembling. He diagnosed a fact, a horrible truth, in its words. The darkness within properly mirrored the darkness he sensed developing within the hearts of his people. They became a disconnect, a growing distance between humanity and the divine, fueled by worry, doubt, and a longing for a simpler time. The inscription, "HaShem Asher Bachar" – The One Who Chooses – echoed in his thoughts, not just as a promise but as a caution. He changed into selected, not to usher in a future of light but to bridge the developing chasm between humanity and the divine. The darkness in the well, a manifestation of their collective anxieties, threatened to engulf them all. He remembered the heavenly City of his early life dreams, a place bathed in light harmony. Now, he noticed that harmony was not bestowed but a delicate stability that needed a steady attempt. The inscription was a key to the beyond and a blueprint for the future – a destiny wherein humanity actively nurtured their reference to the divine, wherein faith changed into protection against the encroaching darkness. Enoch reached out toward the well with a surge of willpower that burned away his worry. Not in a gesture of surrender but with a newfound solution. He would not allow the darkness to win. He might use his presence and connection to the divine to bridge the gap and re-light the flickering flame of religion in human beings' hearts. The well, once a symbol of worry, could become an image of wish – a reminder that even within the face of the deepest darkness, the light of faith may want to triumph.

He woke with a pant, sweat clinging to his skin, the reminiscence of the proper and the chilling voice etched into his mind. It was not just a dream; it became a name for a movement. He would not be a passive observer, looking forward to the darkness to devour them all. He might be a beacon, a bridge, a testament to the iconic energy of religion. The path in advance would not be clean, but with each step and act of kindness and compassion, he would try to heal the disconnect, to steer his human beings back to the light. Enoch starts evolving to look for answers as terrible things continue happening inside the metropolis. A leaden weight settled in Enoch's belly as he rose from his sleep. The dream of the corrupted well lingered, its oily blackness staining his reminiscence with a chilling dread. This was not the first disturbing imagination and prescient that had plagued him in recent nights. The withered fields, the howling wind, and now the contaminated nicely pointed to a future shrouded in darkness, a destiny Enoch was determined to forestall. Once packed with the easy pleasures of village life, his days have been coloured with an undercurrent of fear. He would wander far from his chores, searching for solitude under the old banyan tree where he had first dreamt of the heavenly City. Here, nestled among the gnarled roots, he would pore over the ancient scroll detailing the inscription, "HaShem Asher Bachar" – The One Who Chooses. The inscription, once a melody without music, now held the load of his obligation. He sought out the knowledge of the village elder, a man rumoured to understand forgotten lore. The elder, his weathered face etched with the stories of lifestyles well-lived, listened patiently as Enoch recounted his dreams. He stroked his long, white beard thoughtfully, the silence stretching among them thick with anticipation. Finally, the elder spoke, his voice a low rasp. "These visions," he said, "are not mere figments of wandering thoughts. They are warnings, echoes from destiny whispering of a direction no longer yet taken." Enoch leaned ahead, his heart pounding. "But what route is that? What does the inscription imply?" The elder shook his head. "The meaning of the inscription is misplaced to time. But," he continued, his eyes gleaming with a spark of wish, "the solution lies now not in deciphering phrases but in information and the connection they represent." Enoch's brow furrowed. Understanding the connection? How did that translate to keeping off the darkness he had glimpsed in his dreams? Days changed into weeks as Enoch grappled with the elder's phrases. He discovered his village with a newfound intensity, looking for cracks within the foundation of faith, for any signal of the disconnect the voice within the well had spoken of. He noticed it inside the whispers of discontent about the latest drought, the dwindling attendance on the night prayers, and the growing worry of the unknown that flickered in some eyes. Once trusting and united, the villagers appeared to be drifting aside, their faith in the divine waning beneath the burden of the problem. Enoch realised with a jolt this was the fertile ground wherein the darkness he dreamt of might take root. He needed to act, no longer through grand pronouncements, but with small, kind acts that might reignite the spark of religion within their hearts. He started by helping a widowed woman with her farm chores, his laughter echoing through the fields as he shared the burden of her work. He spent evenings mending nets for the fishers, his testimonies of the heavenly City filling the air with surprise. He prepared games and celebrations to bring the community together and remind them of the strength they saw in team spirit and the solace presented by religion. As the weeks progressed, a diffused shift started out to take location. Smiles lower back to faces, replaced using the concern traces of recent days. Laughter filled the air yet again, a testament to the rejuvenated spirit of the community. Even though not yet a roaring fire, the flickering flame of faith started to burn a little brighter. Enoch knew he had a long road beforehand. The inscription remained a mystery, and the darkness he had glimpsed continued to lurk on the horizon. But for the first time, he was not a witness to the approaching doom. He became a beacon of hope, actively nurturing the relationship between humanity and the divine, building a bridge of faith that might resist any hurricane. The visions nevertheless haunted him, but now they had been not just warnings but a name to action – a reminder that even in the face of the innermost darkness, the energy of religion could light up the direction and manual them toward a brighter destiny. Enoch stood on the precipice of the world, his eyes scanning the horizon for any signal of hope amidst the encroaching darkness. The air changed into heavy with an otherworldly stillness, damaged most effectively through the remote rumble of thunder that echoed like a caution from the heavens themselves. As the primary drops of rain began to fall, Enoch felt a shiver run down his backbone, a coldness that seemed to seep into his very bones. The hurricane clouds loomed overhead, swirling in a sinister dance that painted the sky an ominous colour of black. The earth trembled underneath his toes, the very floor he stood on seeming to groan in protest at the approaching cataclysm. Enoch may want to sense the weight of the sector's sins urgently down on him, a burden that threatened to weigh down his spirit in its enormity. And, amidst the chaos and depression, a flicker of dedication burned vividly inside Enoch's heart. He knew that he could not falter in the face of the darkness that threatened to devour everything he held dear. With every passing second, his resolve strengthened a stealing of his will that set him on a course of unwavering braveness. Enoch raised his voice in solemn prayer as the storm raged around him, calling upon the ancient powers to grant him the electricity and understanding needed to navigate the pains ahead. He knew that the street beforehand might be fraught with danger and uncertainty. Still, he knew he could not afford to waver in his solution. Embracing the strength of the factors, Enoch felt a surge of strength course through his veins, a primal connection to the forces of nature that fueled his spirit and steeled his resolve. With each breath, he drew upon the boundless well of dedication inside him, forging ahead with a feel of a cause that burned like a beacon inside the darkness. With a defiant tilt of his chin, Enoch confronted the storm head-on, his gaze unwavering as he prepared to confront the demanding situations that lay before him. The howling winds buffeted him, the riding rain stinging his skin, but still, he stood strong, a testament to the unyielding strength of his will. And because the storm raged on, the skies above crackling with fury and electricity, Enoch felt calm amidst the chaos. This centeredness anchored him inside the storm's tumultuous embrace. With a quiet willpower that belied the storm's ferocity, he took his first step into the unknown, geared up to confront something trials awaited him with a heart unshaken and a spirit unbroken.

CHAPTER 5: ENOCH'S REVELATION

Terror pricked Enoch's consciousness. Gasping for breath, he sat bolt upright in his bed, the sheets tangled around him. The familiar heady scent of woodsmoke and jasmine that typically greeted him at sunrise suddenly became a thick, acrid stench that clawed at his throat. Panic surged through him because the occasions of his dream unfolded with scary readability. This was not a vision of withered fields or howling winds. This became his village, transformed right into a scene from a nightmare. Flames, like hungry beasts, wolfed the thatched roofs of houses, sending plumes of black smoke into the polluted sky. Screams, each human and animal, pierced the air, a desperate chorus of terror. Enoch stumbled through the dream, his feet crunching on ash and embers. People, their faces contorted in affliction, ran blindly into the inferno, searching for escape from the relentless flames. He noticed acquainted faces – Maya, her darkish hair singed, her eyes huge with terror; Sarah, her once vibrant clothes striking in charred tatters; Ben, his towering form a silhouette towards the flames, his booming laughter changed with the aid of a guttural cough. He reached the village rectangular, the heart in their network now a smouldering pit. The historical banyan tree, beneath which he had spent infinite hours dreaming and sharing memories, lay damaged and useless, its once-proud branches reduced to charred sticks. Above it all, chilling laughter echoed – a sound without joy, packed with malevolent glee. Enoch spun around, trying to find the source of the sound, but saw nothing except a swirling vortex of the fireplace. From its depths, a figure appeared, cloaked in shadows, its eyes glowing like embers. The determined raised a hand, and a wave of searing warmness washed over Enoch. He woke with a scream, the acrid smell of smoke nonetheless clinging to his nostrils, the flavour of worry metal on his tongue. This was not just every other premonition. This became an imaginative and prescient of utter destruction, a chilling glimpse of a destiny where the darkness he had been combating prevailed. Despair threatened to engulf him, the weight of his responsibility crashing down on him. He had tried to bridge the distance, to rebuild religion, but was it enough? Could he, an unmarried man, certainly hold back the tide of darkness that threatened to eat them all? He clutched the worn leather-based pouch around his neck. Inside, nestled against his skin, lay a small, clean stone retrieved from the hidden cave. It pulsed with a faint warm temperature, a comforting reminder of the inscription and the cause it held. He would not succumb to despair. He could combat. The visions had ended up clearer and more urgent. He needed to decipher the inscription and unlock the secrets it held. He needed to discover a way to use his gifts, the relationship to the divine that set him apart, to shield his village from the fiery destiny that awaited them. The inscription, "HaShem Asher Bachar" – The One Who Chooses – whispered a promise, a flicker of wish within the overwhelming darkness. He became selected not simply to convey light but to be the shield against the encroaching flames. With newfound clarity, Enoch rose from his mattress. The sun began peering over the horizon, casting a tentative light at the village that slumbered in peace. He would cherish this peace, this second of innocence, for he knew the darkness would not wait forever. But neither would he. He could be prepared. He will be the bridge, the protector, the one who stood among his village and the fiery abyss that awaited them. People accuse him of being a demon and a danger to the entire town, and the scenario becomes more extreme with each passing day. Dread gnawed at Enoch as he stood before the assembled villagers. The dream of the burning village was fresh in his thoughts, the acrid smoke a phantom sensation in his nostrils. He had to warn them, but the weight of past reports settled heavily on him. Earlier attempts to proportion his visions were met with scepticism, some whispering madness. Taking a deep breath, Enoch acknowledged the scary scene, his voice trembling with urgency. He said the flames, the screams, the chilling laughter that rang through the devastation. An irritating silence punctuated his phrases with fearful coughs and shuffling feet. "It's only a dream," scoffed a weathered farmer named Jebediah, his voice laced with dismissal. "We've all had terrible goals." A murmur of settlement rippled throughout the group. Sarah, her forehead furrowed in concern, advanced. "But Enoch," she began, "your goals regularly..." "Often what?" interrupted a sharp-tongued lady named Esther. "Often carry hassle? Nothing good has happened since he spoke of those extraordinary symbols and his trips to that hidden cave. The drought, the sickness..." Angry whispers erupted, fueled by untold fear and superstition. Enoch felt a chilly dread seep into his bones. He was not supposed to carry fear but to warn them. Yet, his words had served to similarly isolate him. Later that day, as Enoch walked through the market, he felt the load of stares burning into his back. Conversations hushed as he surpassed, replaced through anxious glances and moved quickly to whispers. "Did you hear his loopy tale?" a young woman hissed to her friend. "A demon is coming to break the village, all because of him." "He ought to be cursed," muttered an antique man, shaking his head. "He brings the heavy misfortune." Enoch quickened his pace, the edge of their phrases sharper than any blade. He retreated to the solitude of his room, the inscription on the stone around his neck imparting him scant comfort. He became the selected one, destined to be a bridge. Still, all he regarded to be doing was developing a chasm between himself and his people. Despair threatened to eat him, but then he remembered the warm temperature of the stone, the faint glow that pulsed within. He would not allow fear and suspicion to deter him. He had a cause, a duty. He would find a way to decipher the inscription and bridge the space between humanity and the divine but between himself and his cautious community. He could show them he was their best hope, not a harbinger of doom. Enoch's days have been filled with divine visions and heavenly revelations, each more profound and awe-inspiring than the last. He communed with angels and beheld the mysteries of the heavenly realms, gaining insight into the cosmic order and the divine plan for advent. The weight of his calling bore down on him heavily, but Enoch remained steadfast in his devotion to the Holy One. He preached tirelessly, calling upon all who might pay attention to show from darkness and include the light of fact. Despite dealing with persecution and ridicule, Enoch continued to proclaim the phrase of the Almighty God with unwavering religion and backbone. His message shook the world's rules and stirred the hearts of those who longed for religious fact and enlightenment. Enoch's legacy as a prophet and visionary grew daily as many seekers flocked to pay attention to his words of knowledge and prophecy. He became a guiding light in a world darkened by sin and lack of knowledge, leading endless souls toward righteousness and salvation. And so, Enoch's name became synonymous with divine revelation and spiritual awakening, a beacon of hope for all who looked to realise and understand the mysteries of the universe. His tale would be advised for generations to come back, inspiring souls to look for the presence of the Holy One and walk in the footsteps of the chosen one, Enoch. As Enoch persevered to receive divine revelations, he delved deeper into the mysteries of creation and the designs of the heavenly geographical regions. He changed into showing the complex architecture of the universe, wherein each thread stood for a soul's journey and reason within the grand scheme of life. Enoch's spirit soared to new heights as he beheld the boundless love and mercy of the Almighty God, whose divine plan spread out before him like a heavenly symphony. He saw the dance of the planets and stars, the ebb and glide of time, and the interconnectedness of all living beings within the considerable internet of advent. Through his visions,

Enoch glimpsed the struggles of the angels, the cosmic battles between light and darkness, and the everlasting quest for balance and concord inside the universe. He understood the nature of truth and evil, free will and destiny, and the power of redemption and forgiveness within the eyes of the Holy One. Enoch's heart swelled with gratitude and reverence for the mysteries he was granted to witness, and he longed to share his revelations with all who might concentrate. He spoke eloquently and ardently, his words resonating with the fact and strength of divine knowledge. As Enoch's reputation unfolds some distance and huge, he has become a respected figure among humans, a beacon of light in an international world shrouded in darkness and uncertainty. His teachings guided many souls toward enlightenment and non-secular awakening, igniting a flame of wish and transformation within the hearts of all who heard his message. And so, Enoch's legacy continued to develop, his call whispered in reverence and awe using generations who sought to stroll in the light of the Divine and embrace the everlasting truths revealed through the selected one, Enoch.

CHAPTER 6: THE ANGELS' MESSAGE

As worry and suspicion choked the air like smoke, a sinister plot began to decay inside the hearts of some. Jebediah, the weathered farmer, nursed a grudge against Enoch. He blamed the current hardships – the drought that withered his crops, the contamination that plagued his spouse – on the younger guy's meddling with the unknown. In his superstitious thoughts, Enoch's visions and speech of inscriptions had been not warnings but indications of catastrophe. Esther, the sharp-tongued lady, noticed a possibility to take advantage of the scenario. Power craved a vacuum, and with the villagers increasingly wary of their chief, she saw a risk of manipulating the narrative and seizing manipulation. Enoch was an obstacle, along with his odd gifts and unsettling desires. This unfastened thread threatened to find the underlying cause of the delicate cloth in their network. Then there was Silas, a hulking brute ostracised for his violent temper. He noticed a hazard to redeeming himself within the eyes of the villagers, to finally be visible as a protector instead of a hazard. Enoch and his communication of demons and doom became an easy goal, a scapegoat to be sacrificed for the village's perceived safety. These three, sure through worry, ambition, and a warped experience of duty, met below the cloak of night, their whispers mingling with the rustling leaves. Jebediah, his voice hoarse with conviction, laid out his plan. "He's the blight," he rasped, "the motive for our troubles. We must cleanse the village and rid ourselves of this curse he's added upon us." Esther, her eyes sparkling with chilly ambition, nodded eagerly. "An accident," she purred, "a tragic fall from the cliffs overlooking the hidden cave. No one will suspect an issue." Silas, his face contorted in a grotesque, cool, animated film of righteousness, slammed his fist at the table. "Leave it to me. I'll silence the demon before he can deliver any more harm." Fueled by worry and twisted common sense, their plan hung heavy in the air. In the quiet of the night, a seed of darkness had taken root, threatening to snuff out the delicate wish that also flickered within Enoch's heart. Unaware of the threat that lurked inside the shadows, Enoch persisted in his quest, determined to decipher the inscription and bridge the growing divide within his village, all the even as unknowingly strolling in a direction coated with the whispers of demise. A shaft of moonlight speared through Enoch's thatched roof, illuminating the fear etched on his face. Sleep, a valuable commodity these days, evaded him all over again. The weight of suspicion hung heavy, and the chilling whispers that greeted him at every turn in the village gnawed at his insides. Yet, amidst the depression, a sliver of desire clung to him – the inscription, a flickering ember promising a manner ahead. Suddenly, a blinding light engulfed the room. Enoch flinched, shielding his eyes together with his arm. As the light subsided, a wide-ranging determination materialised earlier than him. Its form became human but celestial, gossamer wings shimmering with an otherworldly luminescence. An experience of awe, laced with a hint of trepidation, washed over Enoch. "Do not be afraid, Enoch," the figure spoke, its voice a melody that resonated inside his very soul. "I am right here to guide you." Enoch stammered, his voice thick with emotion. "Who are you? An angel?" The figure smiled, a radiant warm temperature emanating from its being. "I am a messenger sent to alert you of the darkness that gathers around you." Enoch's heart pounded. "Darkness? Do you suggest the visions? The hearth?" The angel nodded. "But more darkness threatens you presently. Those who fear the unknown, who see your gifts as a curse, plot to silence you." Enoch's breath caught in his throat. The whispers, the cautious glances – they were not simply paranoia. There had been folks who absolutely believed him to be a danger. "You must leave," the angel persevered, its voice laced with urgency. "Flee the village for now, but do no longer melancholy. The inscription holds the key, but its meaning can best be unlocked wherein the light meets the shadow." Enoch's thoughts raced. Where was this near light and shadow? How was he able to decipher the inscription even while on the run? But before he could voice his questions, the angel began to fade. "Seek the Monastery of Whispering Winds," the angel's voice echoed, a whisper at the wind. "There, you may no longer discover the calmest sanctuary, but possibly, the important thing for your cause." With a very last flicker of light, the angel vanished. Enoch sat bolt upright on the mattress, his heart hammering against his ribs. It became a dream, yet it felt actual, a message introduced with the aid of a heavenly being. Fear warned with a newfound willpower. He needed to leave, not out of cowardice, to shield himself and hold his quest. The first rays of dawn painted the sky a pale orange as Enoch shouldered his meagre property. One remaining glance at the village he called domestic, a pang of sadness twisting his gut. He was not forsaking them; he left searching for a way to intercede. With a silent prayer for their safety and a burning remedy in his heart, Enoch went far from the village and began walking, the inscription clutched tightly in his hand, a beacon main him in the direction of the fabled Monastery of Whispering Winds, an area wherein the light met the shadow, and his future awaited. Enoch felt the sector's load on his shoulders as he persisted in his journey, the enormity of the project beforehand of him pressing down on his soul. The angels' messages burned inside him, their phrases a sacred heart that fueled each step. In each village he visited, anybody he spoke to most effectively served to deepen his knowledge of the profound importance of his project. Enoch saw firsthand the depths of humanity's descent into darkness as he travelled. Once colourful cities became overshadowed by corruption and greed, humans were consumed by their personal dreams lying at the feet of others. The sacred legal guidelines of the Great One had been forged apart, replaced by a tradition of selfishness and moral decay. It became a harrowing sight, a stark reminder of the urgent want for repentance and redemption. But amid the despair, Enoch also noticed glimmers of desire. In the eyes of the oppressed and the broken, he diagnosed a longing for something more, a craving for a lifeline to pull them from the abyss. He spoke to them of the angel's message, the promise of forgiveness and renewal that awaited individuals who became lower back to the path of righteousness. His phrases were a beacon of light in an international world shrouded in darkness, presenting a ray of wish in depression. As he journeyed on, Enoch discovered energy in the information that he became no longer by himself in his assignment. The angels watched over him, guiding his steps and empowering his words with divine authority. Their presence became a steady reminder of the sacred belief that had been found upon him, a reminder of the gravity of the message he carried. With each passing day, Enoch felt the urgency of his venture develops ever stronger. The signs and symptoms of the times were turning clearer, the shadows of the coming judgement looming ever larger on the horizon. But he knew he became organised and would face whatever demanding situations lay in advance with unwavering faith and remedy. The destiny of humanity rested on his shoulders, and he might now not falter in his responsibility to deliver the angels' warning to all who could concentrate.

CHAPTER 7: THE HOLY GREAT ONE

The solar beat mercilessly on Enoch's again as he traversed the dusty plains. The weight of the inscription pressed in opposition to his chest was a consistent reminder of his responsibility and the precariousness of his situation. Fear gnawed at the rims of his remedy. Still, the reminiscence of the angel's words, "the Monastery of Whispering Winds," stored him shifting. Days bled into weeks, the panorama reworking from fertile fields to arid scrubland. Hunger gnawed at his belly, and fatigue weighed down his limbs. Yet, with each step, a growing feeling of reason bloomed within him. He was not simply walking from threat; he went on a pilgrimage, a quest to liberate the secrets of the inscription and discover a way to redeem his humans. One particularly starlit night, as exhaustion threatened to weigh him down, he collapsed under the gnarled branches of a lone baobab tree. He cradled the inscription in his palms, his eyes tracing the surprising symbols. Desperation welled up within him.

How might he ever decipher its meaning by me, misplaced in this great wilderness? A light breeze rustled the baobab leaves, and a sizable and effective voice resonated through the night air. It was not the booming voice of his dream on the mountaintop but a voice full of warm temperature and an almost palpable ability. "Enoch," the voice resonated, "do not despair now. You aren't by yourself." Enoch appeared round, his heart pounding. He noticed no person, yet the voice crammed his very being. "The Monastery of Whispering Winds is your vacation spot," the voice persevered, "but it is an insignificant waystation on your adventure. Your genuine route lies beyond the forgotten city of Aethel, wherein the echoes of the divine nonetheless linger." Enoch's breath hitched. Aethel – the heavenly City of his adolescence goals, an area shrouded in delusion and legend. Could it be real or not? "The inscription," the voice explained, "is a fragment of a forgotten language, a key to unlocking the secrets and techniques of Aethel.

Within its walls lies the understanding you are searching for, the route to bridge the chasm between humanity and the divine, and in the end, the salvation of your human beings." A surge of hope jolted Enoch. Aethel, once a fantastical dream, was now a destination, a beacon guiding him on his quest. "But the course is fraught with hazard," the voice warned. "Guardians stand watch, and the shadows that threaten your village will seek to obstruct your development." Enoch steeled himself. He had faced worry before, and he might face it again. He would not let the darkness win. "Remember, Enoch," the voice concluded, a note of encouragement resonating through him, "you bring within you the spark of the divine. Use it to guide you, to protect you, and to light up the direction ahead." As the first rays of dawn kissed the horizon, the voice dwindled. Enoch rose, a newfound determination coursing through him. The inscription was a message and a map leading him to Aethel, the key to saving his human beings. He may also be by myself on the dusty plains, but he was not by myself in spirit. He carried the voice of the Holy Great One within him, a guiding light on his perilous adventure in the direction of redemption. With a renewed feel of cause, Enoch shouldered his % and persisted in his trek, the inscription clutched tightly in his hand, the call Aethel echoing in his heart like a promise. As the sun dipped under the horizon, casting lengthy shadows throughout the land, an experience of awe settled over the humans. They accumulated within the open subject, their eyes turned upward to the heavens, trying to find a signal. And then, inside the distance, a parent regarded. Cloaked in incredible light, radiating a sense of strength and majesty that no one should deny, the Holy Great One stood before them. His presence commanded silence as if the air held its breath in reverence. The people fell to their knees, unable to understand the size of what they had been seeing. The Holy Great One spoke, his voice a booming echo that resonated deep inside their souls. "I am the Alpha and the

Omega, the beginning and the end," he proclaimed. "I am the light inside the darkness, the desire in despair. I am here to guide and expose you to the way." His words crammed them with an experience of peace and knowledge, as though all the questions that had plagued their minds had been suddenly answered. The human beings listened intently, putting on each phrase, knowing they were in the presence of something more than themselves. And because the Holy Great One persevered to talk, his message stuffed their hearts with hope and a renewed sense of reason. They understood that they were not alone regardless of what trials lay in advance. The Holy Great One could constantly be with them, guiding them through the darkness and leading them into the light. The Holy Great One's teachings were profound, delving into the mysteries of the universe and the interconnectedness of all living beings. He said a divine plan, a cosmic order transcending time and area. His words resonated with a truth that touched the very core of their beings, sparking a fireplace of enlightenment inside every character's gift. As the night wore on, the Holy Great One shared tales of historical ability and prophetic visions pointing toward a destiny of peace and concord. His voice carried a weight of authority that inspired awe and reverence, leaving no question inside the minds of those who listened that he became a messenger of the divine. And so, because the stars glittered overhead and the moon solid its silvery glow upon the land, the humans hung on every word of the Holy Great One, their spirits uplifted and their hearts full of a newfound sense of motive and course. They knew they were touched by something more than themselves, something that could guide them on their adventure through the trials and tribulations of existence.

CHAPTER 8: THE COMING FEAR

Days became weeks, then months, with time seeming to rapidly fly by since Enoch had fled the village. He carried the reminiscence of his home, a heavyweight in his heart, as he traversed the unforgiving panorama. News, while it reached him, became like scraps of poisoned bread – every piece an affirmation of his worst fears. Whispers in the wind mentioned a developing drought. The once fertile fields, wherein laughter had mingled with the clinking of hoes, were now barren wastelands, cracked and patched. Once a lifeblood, the property had run dry, its depths echoing with a chilling silence. Hunger gnawed on the villagers' bellies, and depression has become a consistent associate. But the drought became severe at the start. Sickness, a virulent plague whispered to be born of the darkness Enoch had dreamt of, swept through the village. Once vibrant and full of life, children lay listless in their beds, their coughs echoing like mournful cries amidst the abandoned streets. Even Sarah, the female who had continually believed in Enoch's visions, succumbed, her kind eyes clouded with fever before dimming all the time. The whispers in opposition to Enoch escalated to accusations. Esther's ambition festering within the fertile floor of worry fueled the flames. "He introduced this curse upon us!" she would shriek, her voice laced with venom. "With his darkish visions and communication of demons, he angered the gods!" Jebediah, consumed by grief for his spouse, easily echoed her phrases. "He is a monster, a blight!" he roared, his voice thick with a grief that had morphed right into a risky rage. Once pillars of ability, the elders retreated into a shell of fear and indecision. With their leader gone and no clear course ahead, the cloth of the village began to unravel. Accusations became threats, and shortly after, violence erupted. Silas, the brute who had plotted Enoch's loss of life, determined a new motive – becoming Esther's enforcer, silencing any dissent with brutal performance. The once nonviolent village, bathed within the heat glow of community, was now a husk of its former self. Hatred and worry simmered in the air, a toxic brew poisoning the very souls of its inhabitants. News of this descent into chaos reached Enoch through a travelling peddler, a gaunt guy with eyes that reflected the desolation he defined. Enoch clutched the inscription, his knuckles white. Every fibre of his being screamed to return, stand the effects of his preference, and guard his people. But the voice of the Holy Great One echoed in his thoughts, a steady reminder – Aethel held the key. Only by carrying out the forgotten town and unlocking the secrets of the inscription may he want to save his people from the encroaching darkness. The adventure seemed more daunting than ever. The weight of his village's suffering pressed down on him, a darkish counterpoint to the desire the voice of the Holy Great One had instilled. Yet, amidst the depression, a flicker of defiance remained. He would not allow the darkness to win. He would reach Aethel, decipher the inscription, and return, not as a fugitive but as a saviour, equipped to bridge the chasm that had added his beloved village to its knees. The road in advance became fraught with peril, but the fate of his humans hung within the stability. With a heavy heart and a resolute spirit, Enoch pressed on to the forgotten city of Aethel, his most effective hope. Enoch's pilgrimage towards Aethel became a grim adventure ridden with unsettling despair. The once colourful stories shared by wandering merchants had been replaced by hollow whispers and vacant stares. Each metropolis he met seemed to be a microcosm of the destruction festering in his village, a grim reflection of the darkness spreading throughout the land. In the primary city, a once bustling marketplace rectangular lay deserted. Dust devils danced throughout the cracked earth, mocking the empty stalls and shuttered windows. The air hung heavy with a silence broken by the mournful creaking of a climate-overwhelmed sign. Here, the darkness manifested as a constant sandstorm. This suffocating shroud choked plants and choked the lifestyles out of the land. The few remaining villagers, their faces etched with depression, referred to when the sky became blue, and the wind carried the scent of rain. Now, they awaited a gradual, agonising dying, their religion within the divine buried beneath the relentless dunes. Enoch lingered for a day, presenting what little he had – memories from his early life, songs of desire and resilience. But the spark in their eyes remained extinguished. Once a colourful flame, their connection to the divine had dwindled into bloodless ash. He left with a heavy heart, and the image in their hollow stares was a stark reminder of the destiny that awaited his personal village if he failed. The next city becomes a stark comparison. Here, the air crackled with feverish electricity. People moved with frantic haste, their eyes glowing with manic desperation. Once fertile fields surrounding the town became a community of trenches, the villagers clawed on the earth in a determined search for water. Once a supply of life, the well had run dry, its depths echoing with the clinking of pickaxes and the determined pleas of the thirsty. The darkness of this city wore the mask of greed. It had poisoned their faith, twisting their connection to the divine right into an egocentric scramble for survival. They noticed the dwindling water as a finite aid, a prize to be fought over instead of a shared blessing. Enoch saw households torn aside, friendships shattered, enthusiastic about some treasured drops of the life-giving liquid. He spent his time right here not with testimonies but with actions. He helped dig, shared his meagre rations, and tried vainly to motivate those consumed by their thirst for survival. By the time he left, the city was at the point of open conflict. Armed guards patrolled the water rations, and the once cheery greetings have been replaced with suspicious glares and muttered threats. The darkness here had taken root not within the earth but within the hearts of men, a chilling testament to the negative power of unchecked fear and desperation. Enoch's adventure has become a litany of suffering. Each city, with its specific emblem of depression, chipped away at his hope. Yet, with every come upon, his clear-up hardened. He had seen firsthand the devastating consequences of a broken connection between humanity and the divine. He would not allow his village to go through an equal fate. He pressed on toward Aethel, the load of his responsibility a steady burden, but the reminiscence of the Holy Great One's voice, a flickering ember guiding him through the collection darkness. As the night deepened, casting its inky shadows over the village of Kaldor, the whispered premonitions of approaching doom grew louder, haunting the villagers' minds like spectres inside the mist. Enoch, the venerable sage, stood along with his eyes constant on the horizon, his heart heavy with the burden of what he knew changed into to come back. The air was thick with anxiety, every breath laced with unease that seemed to seep into the village's soil. The flickering torches that covered the rectangular forged dancing shadows on the weather-crushed faces of the collected villagers, their eyes reflecting the inner turmoil that gripped them all. Enoch raised his voice again, his phrases cutting through the silence like a blade. "My pals," he intoned, his voice consistent and resolute, "we stand on the precipice of a darkness that threatens to consume us all. But recollect, in trial instances, our solidarity shall be our best strength. Let us not succumb to fear, but alternatively, allow us to find solace in one another, for collectively, we can resist even the darkest of nights." The villagers exchanged wary glances, the gravity of Enoch's words sinking deep into their souls. They knew the days ahead could look at their mettle in approaches they had not imagined. But inside the sage's steadfast gaze, they found a glimmer of hope, a spark of braveness that kindled a fire in their hearts. As the last embers of daylight diminished into the velvety darkness of night, a feeling of sombre determination settled over the village. They stood shoulder to shoulder, certain with a common purpose and an unstated vow to stand something trials lay in advance with unwavering clear up. So, within the quiet stillness of the night, the villagers of Kaldor braced themselves for the unknown, their collective spirit a beacon of light amidst the encroaching shadows of uncertainty. The ancient timber surrounding the village whispered secrets of times long past, their gnarled branches achieving out like bony palms clawing on the veil among the dwellings of the lifeless. The night became alive with a palpable foreboding feel, as though the land itself mourned the approaching darkness. Enoch and his years of ability etched into the strains of his weathered face knew that the omens had been proper. An amazing evil lurked on the horizon, a force that threatened to eat everything in its direction. The weight of responsibility pressed heavily upon his shoulders, the weight of shielding his people from the unknown. But amidst the concern and uncertainty, a flicker of defiance burned vividly in Enoch's eyes. He could not stand idly by while the darkness descended upon his home. With a feeling of because that cut through the shadows like a sword, he came to the villagers again, his voice ringing out unwavering remedy. "We can be but easy folks, but we are certain together by bonds more potent than metallic," Enoch declared, his phrases carrying a weight that resonated inside the hearts of all who heard them. "Though the road ahead can be fraught with peril, realise this - as long as we stand united, we are unconquerable." The villagers nodded in silent agreement, their faces determined as they prepared to stand the trials that awaited them. In the stillness of the night, an experience of team spirit washed over the village, a shared dedication to climate the storm together, no matter what happens. And so, as the moon rose excessively inside the sky, casting a silvery glow over the panorama, the villagers of Kaldor stood as one, a beacon of resilience and desire within the face of the encroaching darkness.

CHAPTER 9: THE QUAKING WATCHERS

The relentless sun beat down Enoch's lower back, turning his sweat to salt on his solar-baked pores and skin. His journey had stretched on for what felt like an eternity, every encounter with a ravaged metropolis a clean wound on his spirit. Yet, with each problem, the inscription in his hand pulsed with a faint warm temperature, a beacon reminding him of his cause. Finally, after weeks of trudging along an unforgiving terrain, the panorama shifted. A cluster of weathered sandstone mesas, their flat tops catching the afternoon light, rose from the plains like silent sentinels. As Enoch drew closer, a gasp escaped his lips. Nestled among the mesas, hidden by wind-sculpted dunes, lay the ruins of an extraordinary temple complex. Carvings depicting heavenly beings embellished the crumbling facades, their once colourful colourations muted by time. Hieroglyphs, just like the symbols at the inscription, snaked across the weathered stones, whispering secrets in a forgotten tongue. This became it. This needed to be a place where the inscription may finally reveal its secrets, a gateway to the knowledge he desperately sought. A surge of excitement coursed through him, momentarily erasing the weariness that had turned out to be his regular associate. With renewed vigour, he quickened his tempo, his boots crunching at the shifting sand as he ascended towards the temple complex. The closer he got, the more the immensity of the location crushed him. Despite its grandeur, this place emanated a charisma of forgotten strength, an experience of secrets nicely left undisturbed. The air hung heavy with an unsettling silence, damaged simply by the mournful sigh of the wind whistling through the ruins. Enoch hesitated at the doorway, a tremor of apprehension running through him. Despite its grandeur, this place emanated a charisma of forgotten strength, an experience of secrets nicely left undisturbed. But the idea of his village and his people's desperate pleas echoing in his mind propelled him forward. He entered the gaping maw of the entrance, getting into a big hall bathed in celestial twilight. Sand covered the floor in a thick layer, swallowing the problematic designs that adorned it. Statues, their expressions weathered and stoic, gazed down from their pedestals, silent guardians of a forgotten age. In the centre of the corridor, a large stone pedestal held a single, weathered object – a huge, round disc included within the equal swirling symbols because of the inscription. Enoch's heart pounded in his chest. This needed to be the important thing. This became the answer he had been looking for. With trembling fingers, he approached the pedestal. The inscription in his hand seemed to thrum with a newfound electricity, resonating with the symbols on the disc. A wave of dizziness washed over him as he reached out to touch it. The air shimmered, and the acquainted surroundings dissolved into a kaleidoscope of swirling colours. When his vision cleared, Enoch determined his status in a one-of-a-kind chamber, smaller and more intimate than the grand corridor. The partitions have been adorned with complex works depicting heavenly beings interacting with humans, a testament to a time when the relationship between humanity and the divine became sturdy. But amidst the colourful work of art, an uncanny picture sent a jolt of fear through him. It depicted an enormous parent, its form wreathed in shadow, its eyes glowing with malevolent hunger. And underneath it, scrawled inside the same language because the inscription had been phrases that sent a chill down his spine: "The Broken Covenant." Enoch's breath hitched. The darkness he had been preventing and the visions that had plagued him were not mere nightmares. As a result, they were a reminder of a broken relationship between humanity and the divine. The inscription, the disc, the very knowledge he looked for – all held the key to saving his village and mending a fractured courting that threatened to engulf the sector in darkness. The weight of this revelation settled closely on his shoulders. He was not only a pilgrim on a private quest; he became a bridge between two worlds, a bearer of a reality that might rewrite the direction of history. With a newfound determination, Enoch approached the murals to delve deeper into the secrets and techniques they held, to recognise the nature of the damaged covenant and, hopefully, find a way to fix it. The destiny of his village and the sector itself relied on it. He meets the watchers, who are speculated to scare human beings from getting access to the temple, but they may also be terrified. Disoriented and blinking away at the afterimages of the swirling colours, Enoch saw himself in a smaller chamber. Gone was the widespread emptiness of the entrance corridor; as an alternative, the gap became intimate, adorned with murals that shimmered with an otherworldly luminescence. But earlier than he ought to completely take it in, a bone-chilling voice echoed through the room. "Who dares trespass on the sacred floor?" Enoch whirled around, his hand instinctively reaching the dagger strapped to his thigh. Two figures materialised from the shadows, their forms tall and enforcing. Cloaked in shimmering gowns regarded to take in the light around them, they emanate an unsettling charisma of strength. Their faces had been obscured through hoods, leaving the most effective swimming pools of darkness in which eyes ought to be. "Who are you?" Enoch asked, his voice barely a whisper. "We are the Watchers," the primary determination boomed, the voice resonating like thunder in the constrained space. "Guardians of this temple and keepers of forbidden knowledge." Enoch's heart pounded in his chest. These have been the

Watchers, the very beings from his dreams who had fallen from grace. Fear threatened to paralyse him, but the reminiscence of his suffering village spurred him on. "I come looking for understanding," he stammered, forcing himself to meet the unseen gaze of the Watchers. "Knowledge to keep my humans."

The second Watcher scoffed, the sound sharp and dismissive. "Mortals have no want of such understanding. It brings the simplest chaos." "But the darkness spreads," Enoch pleaded. "My village… my global… they may be on the point of destruction. The inscription… the disc… they keep the solutions, don't they?" A disturbing silence saw his question. The Watchers sought advice from each other in a language that gave the impression of wind rustling through ancient trees. Finally, the primary Watcher spoke. "The inscription holds the key to a power beyond your comprehension," he said, his voice laced with caution. "An energy that could bring salvation or annihilation." "I recognise the dangers," Enoch pressed, "but I haven't any preference. My humans go through, and I must assist them." The Watchers persevered in their silent exchange, the tension inside the chamber thickening with every passing moment. Finally, they stepped apart, revealing the murals on the wall. "Very nicely," the primary Watcher conceded, his voice like gravel grinding towards the stone. "But be warned, mortal. The knowledge you are looking for comes at a steep price. Are you prepared to pay for it?" Enoch starred in the work of art, the weight of their words settling closely on him. He knew the route beforehand would not be smooth. There might be trials to stand, secrets to uncover, and even risks past his wildest imagination. Yet, the picture of his village, ravaged by drought and melancholy, flashed in his thoughts.

"I don't have any different desire," he said, his voice firm despite the tremor in his heart. "I need to shop for my people." With a nod, the Watchers vanished as silently as they had regarded. Enoch stood by himself before the murals, their complex information now pulsating with celestial light. The actual undertaking, the price of the forbidden information he was chasing, lay hidden within the secrets whispered by the work of art of the temple. Taking a deep breath, Enoch advanced, equipped to stand something. Trials awaited him, his remedy fueled by the desperate desire to bring redemption to his village and light to an international teetering ready for darkness.

Enoch stood at the threshold of the intimidating terrain, his heart heavy with foreboding. The earth rumbled underneath his feet, a caution of impending doom. The watchers, fallen angels who had once been entrusted with guarding humanity, now trembled with worry. Their once proud and defiant demeanour had crumbled into a pitiful show of desperation and regret. Enoch ought to see the torment etched in their faces, the weight of their imminent judgement bearing upon them like a crushing burden. But amid the chaos and worry, a faint glimmer of desire appeared to flicker in their eyes. Enoch, the trustworthy scribe, felt a profound experience of empathy for those fallen beings. He understood the seductive appeal of power and the harmful nature of pride, for he had seen it corrupt even the largest noble of beings. And so, as he stood at the precipice and saw the trembling watchers, a prayer of compassion and forgiveness rose from his soul. He prayed to the Holy Great One, the creator of all matters, to reveal mercy and grace to folks who had lost their way. Enoch's voice sounded clear and robust, a beacon of wish amid impending judgment. At that moment, a profound feeling of peace settled over him, a reassurance that even inside the face of darkness, the light of divine forgiveness shone brightest. Enoch's prayer resonated with the chaos as the earth persevered to quake, and the watchers trembled, supplying a glimmer of redemption in a sea of fear. In that sacred second, he knew that irrespective of the depths of depression, the boundless love of the holy one usually became there, equipped to manual lost souls that returned to the route of righteousness. The wind whipped around Enoch, wearing the echoes of ancient prophecies and whispered secrets and techniques. He felt like he stood at the crossroads of time, witnessing the everlasting conflict between light and darkness. The electricity of the heavens crackled inside the air, filling Enoch with a feeling of divine motive. An unmarried tear rolled down Enoch's cheek, a tear shed for the fallen watchers and all of humanity trapped with the aid of sin. he knew that during this moment of reckoning, the destiny of the arena hung inside the stability, teetering on the brink of destruction or redemption. As he gazed into the depths of eternity, Enoch understood that his position as a scribe had changed, and he was no longer merely transcribing the phrases of the divine but encompassing the compassion and mercy that flowed from the heart of the holy one. With a steadfast clear-up, Enoch raised his voice again, an emotional plea for salvation and renewal. The heavens considered preserving their breath, awaiting the verdict shaping history. In that charged ecosystem of hysteria and desire, Enoch stood as a beacon of lightness within the encroaching darkness, a vessel of grace and forgiveness in an international world on the brink of chaos.

CHAPTER 10: TREMBLING ENDS

Enoch, heart hammering towards his ribs like a trapped bird, stepped toward the pulsating murals. The Watchers' caution echoed in his mind — the price of understanding may be steep. He braced himself for a bodily undertaking, a few magical barriers or a fiery onslaught. But as a substitute, the very foundation of the temple started to tremble. A low rumble echoed through the chamber, increasing with each passing second. Dust rained from the ceiling, and the murals swayed precariously on the partitions. Panic clawed at Enoch's throat. Was this the price the Watchers had spoken of? Was he being punished for his audacity? Suddenly, the tremor escalated right into a full-blown earthquake. The ground heaved under his toes, and the air crackled with a low electric hum. Sand and debris rained down from the crumbling ceiling, forcing Enoch to defend his face with his arm. He stumbled backwards, desperately seeking a cowl under a crumbling pillar. The room became a cacophony of crashing stone and his ragged respiratory. Through the dust and particles, he could see the once-colourful work of art fracturing, their secrets always misplaced. A primal scream tour from his throat, a valid mingled fear and frustration. He had come to this point, continued trouble after worry, and was simplest to have the knowledge he looked for destroyed earlier than his eyes. Despair threatened to engulf him. He had failed. His adventure, his hope for his village – taken with nothing. But then, as his eyes adjusted to the dim light filtering the dust cloud, he saw a shift. A segment of the ground, formerly obscured by a now fallen piece of masonry, lay uncovered. It was not stone but a clean, obsidian-like floor that shimmered with an otherworldly light. Curiosity momentarily eclipsing his depression, Enoch cautiously approached. As he drew closer, a faint inscription materialised at the surface, sparkling with the same depth as his inscription's symbols. It pulsed with a faint warm temperature, an invitation instead of a caution. Could this be a brand-new course, a one-of-a-kind way to access the knowledge he sought? Hope, like a flickering ember, rekindled within him. The Watchers' trial could also have taken a surprising shape, a terrifying display of uncooked strength that threatened to bury him alive. But hopefully, it was not a lifeless surrender. This inscription, this obsidian portal, held the important thing of unlocking the secrets and techniques of the temple, the important thing of saving his village. With a newfound determination, fueled by the aid of a sliver of hope that refused to be extinguished, Enoch knelt before the inscription, his hand hovering over the glowing symbols. He had come too far to return now. He could face some challenges awaiting him, decipher the secrets and techniques of this new inscription, and find a way to bridge the chasm between humanity and the divine, even supposing it meant venturing down a route as unknown and threatening as the one that had just shaken the very foundation of the temple. The inscription pulsed underneath his touch, a warm temperature spreading from his fingertips up his arm. He closed his eyes, the picture of his parched and determined village flashing in his mind. This was not just for him anymore. This became for Sarah, his kindhearted neighbour, her light eyes now clouded by fever. This saw Jebediah turn from a once proud farmer to a man now eaten up by grief and rage. This became his complete village, teetering on the point of destruction. He took a deep breath, the burden of obligation settling heavily on his shoulders. He now becomes not just an easy villager but a bearer of hope, a bridge among worlds. With a newfound clear up, Enoch began to trace the symbols of the inscription, his voice a low murmur as he spoke the phrases inside the forgotten language, the language whispered by using the voice of the Holy Great One. The air crackled with energy, and the obsidian ground hummed beneath him. He did not understand where this route could lead but knew he needed to keep going. The destiny of his world trusted it. Enoch's voice rang out across the land, his words a haunting melody that stirred the souls of individuals who listened. As the echoes of his prophecy diminished into the night, a hushed silence fell upon the people, a heavy weight of anticipation and worry settling in their hearts. They knew Enoch's visions would no longer be taken gently, for they bore the burden of fact and knowledge that transcended mortal ability. In the distance, a lone wolf howled mournfully, its cry carried at the wind like a lament for the arena itself. The night sky above shimmered with an array of stars, each a silent witness to the events unfolding beneath. Enoch stood as a solitary figure in opposition to the great expanse of darkness, his form illuminated with the aid of an internal lightness that defied the shadows that threatened to engulf all of them. The ground under Enoch's toes started to crack and fissure as though the earth began rebelling in opposition to his words. The people gasped in horror, feeling the tremors of unrest ripple through their very beings. Yet Enoch remained steadfast, his eyes fixed on a distant horizon that promised a brand-new sunrise beyond the encroaching darkness. With a voice that carried the load of millennia, Enoch persevered with his prophecy, carrying the inexplicable burden of destiny and destiny that intertwined the lives of all who stood before him. He pointed out a time of top-notch upheaval, when the antique approaches would be forged apart, and a brand-new order would thrust upward from the ashes of the beyond. He noted a delegated few, destined to play a pivotal function within the unfolding drama of introduction, their destinies intertwined with the threads of time. As Enoch's deep, powerful voice reached a crescendo, a blinding light erupted from the heavens, bathing the land in a divine radiance that pierced the veil of night. The human beings shielded their eyes, overwhelmed by the sheer power and majesty of the heavenly show. And in that second of awe and wonder, they felt their souls stirring, a glimmer of wish that shone like a beacon within the darkness. Enoch diminished his hands, the light fading from his eyes as he turned to face the human beings again. His gaze became a profound unhappiness, a burden of knowledge that weighed closely upon his historic shoulders. And there was also a flicker of remedy, a dedication that burned shiny inside the depths of his being. He knew that the advanced course could be fraught with peril and uncertainty, but he also knew that inside the hearts of the people lay the energy to rise above their fears and doubts. And as the night closed in around them, Enoch raised his voice one remaining time, his phrases a name to arms, a rallying cry for all who dared to dream of a world reborn.

Chapter 11: The Lost Word

The temple trembled anew, but the tremor felt less damaging and extra… functional this time. The light emanating from the obsidian ground intensified, pulling Enoch into its warm glow. He squeezed his eyes close, the forgotten language of the Holy Great One cascading from his lips like a forgotten melody. He felt himself lifted, his body dissolving into the light, the inscriptions on the obsidian floor blurring into a kaleidoscope of swirling symbols. When he opened his eyes, the world around him had shifted. He changed into now, not within the crumbling chamberlain but in a tremendous, celestial area filled with swirling stardust and shimmering nebulae. A parent, made of lightness, stood earlier than him, its radiance so intense he should slightly look at it at once. "Enoch," the discern boomed, the voice resonating like the chime of one thousand heavenly bells. "You have come a long way." Enoch fell to his knees, beaten by the presence before him. "Holy Great One," he stammered, the voice that had haunted his desires for goodbye now a comforting presence, "I... I am trying to find the knowledge to shop in my village." The parent pulsed with a celestial light. "Knowledge on my own will not be your salvation, Enoch. It would be best if you also rediscovered the misplaced connection between humanity and the divine, the broken covenant. Enoch's heart pounded. The covenant! That was the picture he had glimpsed within the mural, the supply of the darkness plaguing his international. "The inscription you keep," the Holy Great One endured, its voice devoid of judgement, "is a fragment of this covenant, a reminder of the language once used to talk with the divine. It is important to restore stability." Enoch clutched the inscription close to his chest. "But how? The Watchers—" The Holy Great One silenced him with a gesture of its luminous hand. "The Watchers are sure guardians but also testaments to the consequences of a broken covenant. Their energy wanes as humanity forgets how to speak the divine language, a way to get admission to the power living inside." A wave of knowledge washed over Enoch. The Watchers were not demons; they were fallen beings, their connection to the divine severed. Their worry stemmed no longer from malice but from a desperate loneliness, a longing for a connection they had misplaced. "The misplaced phrases," Enoch rasped, "the words I heard in my visions... are they the phrases of the covenant?" The Holy Great One pulsed with a warm light. "Indeed, Enoch. You can become a bridge, a conduit between the human and the divine. By unlocking the misplaced phrases, you can understand the inscription and its power and start to mend the fractured covenant."

Enoch's mind reeled. He was not just a bearer of information but an able peacemaker, a bridge between two worlds teetering on the brink of war. The duty weighed closely on him, but it also became a glimmer of hope, a path closer to redemption. In the celestial space, the Holy Great One started to talk, a symphony of light and comforting sound filling the void. Enoch listened, his entire being absorbing the forgotten language, the misplaced phrases of the covenant echoing inside him. It changed into a language no longer of human phrases but of feelings, natural strength, and a manner to communicate simultaneously with the divine. As the lesson opened, Enoch saw visions flash of things that preceded the existence of his eyes, not mere recollections but an illustrious representation of a bygone generation. He noticed a time when humanity and the divine co-existed, an international bath in harmony in which heavenly beings and women and men walked side by side. He saw the fracturing of the covenant, a misunderstanding that led to worry and separation. He saw the Watchers fall from grace, their connection severed, their power waning with each passing era. He noticed the direction to mending it – a direction paved with ability, compassion, and the reawakening of a dormant connection. When the lesson ended, Enoch fell silent, the load of the ability settling closely on him. The forgotten language echoed within him, a dormant strength waiting to be unleashed. It was not just knowledge; it became a responsibility, a burden he now bore with the quiet strength of a man chosen for a reason some distance more than himself.

"Now, Enoch," the Holy Great One said, its voice filled with a warm temperature that touched his soul, "pass forth. Use your newfound knowledge, bridge the chasm, and permit harmony to reign again." The world around Enoch dissolved into light another time, after which... he saw himself lower back in the crumbling chamberlain, the inscription clutched tight in his hand. The tremors had subsided, and an eerie silence had descended. The air crackled with newfound strength, reacting to the phrases now resonating within him. Enoch stood tall, a unique, modified man. The inscription in his hand felt not like parchment but a dwelling element, pulsing with the strength of the forgotten language. The visions he had seen inside celestial space were not simply reminiscences; they had been a raw, emotional rollercoaster depicting the vibrant connection between humanity and the divine and the chilling motive for its dying. As he stood there, bathed in the celestial afterglow of his revel, the Holy Great One's voice echoed in his thoughts, a whisper tinged with profound sorrow. "The fracturing of the covenant... a misunderstanding that led to worry..." Enoch closed his eyes, the visions flashing before him all over again, but this time with a deeper clarity. He noticed now not simply the beauty of a bygone era but the subtle cracks that had all started to spiderweb across the once-unified globe. Greed and ambition, like insidious weeds, had taken root inside fellows' hearts to petty conflicts and a simmering resentment toward the divine. A single picture burned into Enoch's mind with specific intensity – a human chief, fed on by using energy and blinded by using his own self-significance, difficult the information of a heavenly being. Arrogance and delight twisted his features, his phrases laced with accusations and thinly veiled disrespect. The heavenly being, once a benevolent manual, recoiled in unhappiness. A tremor ran through the world, a physical manifestation of the fracturing bond. Enoch gasped. It was not a singular, dramatic betrayal that had severed the relationship but a sluggish, agonising erosion of consideration. The language of feelings, once a bridge of ability, had become a weapon of misunderstanding. Humans, unable to understand the divine perspective, misinterpreted guidance as manipulation. The divine, hurt by the developing distrust, retreated, their communication reduced to cryptic warnings and infrequent interventions. A chilling consciousness dawned on Enoch. The darkness plaguing his world was not a demonic entity hell-bent on destruction; it became the absence of the divine light. With the covenant damaged, the sector was left susceptible to a lawn without its caretaker. The drought, sickness, and rising chaos were all symptoms of global starvation and the stability the divine presence once nurtured. Despair threatened to engulf him. How should he, a single man, mend the sort of large chasm? But then, a flicker of the Holy Great One's warm temperature filled him. They had not despatched him again empty-exceeded. He had the forgotten language, the key to reopening the door of conversation, a bridge built not of stone and mortar but of information and empathy.

Hope surged through him, albeit tinged with trepidation. He would not simply be bridging a gap but navigating a minefield of suspicion and resentment. Humans, hardened by using fear and problem, might not effectively take delivery of a message added in a language lengthy forgotten. But he needed to strive. The destiny of his village, even the sector, trusted it. Enoch stepped out of the chamber with newfound clarity, the inscription a beacon of possibility in his hand. The forgotten language was not a weapon of battle but a tool for understanding, a risk to construct a bridge from the shattered remnants of trust. He knew the journey in advance would be fraught with threats. Still, the alternative – a nation eaten up by darkness, a people driven mad by worry and desperation – was unthinkable. He had a message to supply, now not just to his village but to all of humanity: the darkness was not an enemy to fight but a void to fill with the forgotten language of the covenant, a language of solidarity, admiration, and understanding. Only then should the light go back and hope for a world on the point of falling into despair. The road in advance was long and unsure. Still, Enoch, armed with the ability of the past and the energy of the forgotten language, became not only an easy villager. He became a bridge between worlds, a bearer of wish, and the last chance for a global teetering on the brink of oblivion. His adventure had simply all started, and the fate of humanity hinged on his achievement. Enoch met various demanding situations and obstacles as he embarked on his mission to share the lost word with the world. The course was now not smooth, fraught with sceptics and naysayers who doubted the electricity of his message. But Enoch remained steadfast in his notion, drawing energy from the deep well of ability revealed to him. Enoch mentioned the lost word and its profound importance when travelling from village to village. He saw transformative results of his phrases, as people's hearts were touched and their spirits were uplifted. His message resonated with a protracted-forgotten reminiscence buried deep within every soul, awakening an experience of divine connection that had long been dormant. But as Enoch delved deeper into his quest, he began to feel a developing darkness lurking on the horizon. Whispers of discord and department echoed inside the wind, threatening to overshadow the concord and solidarity he looked to sell. It became clear to Enoch that he must confront this darkness head-on, armed with the electricity of the misplaced phrase and the unwavering conviction in its fact. At the edge of a large chasm, wherein the shadows clung like veils of melancholy, Enoch faced the embodiment of this darkness – a being of evil reason, twisted and suffering from its personal internal turmoil. With a consistent gaze and a heart filled with compassion, Enoch reached out to the being, presenting the light of the misplaced phrase as a beacon of desire in darkness. In that second connection, something shifted within the being. A glimmer of reputation flickered in its eyes, and its twisted form began to soften and find the underlying cause of it. As the lost phrase resonated through the chasm, it became like a bell had been rung, heralding a brand-new era of knowledge and reconciliation. Enoch watched in awe as the being transformed earlier than his eyes, losing its darkness like a cocoon to reveal the radiant essence at its core. In that second of profound revelation, Enoch understood the actual electricity of the lost phrase – now not just as a way of cohesion but as a catalyst for transformation and healing on a cosmic scale. With a heart overflowing with gratitude and humility, Enoch persevered on his journey, knowing that the truest strength lay no longer in his words but inside the goal and love that infused them. And as he travelled onward, the misplaced word's echoes reverberated through the cosmos, weaving a delicately intricate connection and concord that transcends all barriers and divisions.

CHAPTER 12: THE CALL OF ENOCH

"My children," boomed the voice of the Holy One, a legitimate voice that resonated with the power of creation itself. "Darkness descends upon the world of mortals. Greed and delight have fractured the covenant, and humanity walks a dangerous direction shrouded in worry." A murmur rippled among the angels. Seraph, her wings aglow with the purest white light, improved. "What becomes of them, Holy One? Will they be fed on by using the shadows they have birthed?" "Not if there is a wish," the Holy One replied, his voice full of historic disappointment. "A bridge must be built, a conduit among the heavenly and the earthly realms. A soul pure of heart and unwavering in religion is needed to carry this burden." A younger angel, Michael, with vibrant blue wings, spoke up. "But who, Holy One? Who can stroll among mortals and remind them of the light?" The Holy One's gaze swept through the heavenly expanse, selecting a radiant parent bathed in a soft, golden light. It became Raphael, the angel of healing, his presence emanating warmth and compassion. "Raphael," the Holy One spoke, his voice gentle, "appearing upon the village of Aijalon. There, a baby is ready to be born among the simple folks. His call shall be Enoch; within him is living the spark of ability – a potential to bridge the chasm between humanity and the divine."

Raphael bowed low. "As you command, Holy One. I shall watch over Enoch, manual his steps, and nurture the light within him." And so, it got here to bypass. On a night bathed inside the gentle glow of heavenly light, Enoch changed into born. Raphael, unseen by mortal eyes, hovered near the cradle, his presence a silent mum or dad as the child drew his first breath. Throughout his adolescence, Raphael subtly nudged Enoch closer to kindness, compassion, and a deep recognition of the natural world. He whispered stories of the forgotten concord between humanity and the divine, planting seeds of desire inside the younger boy's heart.

Years passed, and Enoch grew into a man, a pillar of his network recognised for his knowledge and unwavering religion. He was not without his flaws – a touch of stubbornness, a tendency to wear his heart on his sleeve. But these imperfections had been overshadowed by his authentic empathy and unwavering feeling of humanity's inherent goodness. One fateful night, as depression gripped Aijalon, the Holy One's voice echoed in Enoch's dreams, a name to motion that resonated with the essence of his being. The goals had been bright, full of scenes of a withering international and a fractured sky, a stark reminder of the results of the broken covenant. Raphael, ever-present, saw Enoch's war. The burden placed upon him turned heavy, the course beforehand fraught with risk. It would require Enoch to mission beyond his village's acquainted consolation, confront the darkness head-on, and free up secrets and techniques deep inside the world's forgotten corners. Yet, Raphael noticed the flicker of willpower in Enoch's eyes. This unwavering religion resonated with the light nurtured within him because of his delivery. "He is prepared," Raphael declared to the Holy One, his voice full of satisfaction. "Enoch will answer the call. He will adventure to the forgotten locations, unlock the secrets of the past, and remind humanity of the light within them." The Holy One smiled, a radiant warm temperature spreading through the heavenly realm. "Then permit his adventure to start. May he discover the strength to bridge the chasm and bring a new harmony technology between the heavens and the earth." And so, with the blessings of the Holy One and the watchful presence of his father or mother angel, Enoch launched into his quest. His birth, a testament to the iconic wish of the divine, marked the start of an adventure that would decide the fate of a world teetering on the threshold of darkness. The chosen one, nurtured by unseen fingers and guided through the whispers of the heavenly realm, walked toward a destiny that might redefine the relationship between humanity and the divine. This changed into no everyday pilgrimage. Enoch would not be traversing familiar paths or meeting pleasant faces. His journey might check him in methods he could not believe, forcing him to confront the simplest darkness plaguing the sector and the darkness within himself. Yet, inside him burned the spark of the Holy One's light, a beacon of wish that could guide him through the coming trials. He became humanity's bridge, their champion, and their final chance at redemption. The destiny of his international career rested on his shoulders, a daunting and exhilarating duty. As Enoch stepped out into the unknown, a tremor vibrated through the earth, a bodily manifestation of the influential project earlier than him. He clutched the inscription, the parchment now imbued with a faint warm temperature. Raphael's voice echoed in his thoughts – a light reminder of the forgotten language, the key to unlocking past secrets. His journey would not be a solitary one. Seraph, the angel of wisdom, could manipulate him with cryptic messages and forgotten lore. She could appear as a raven, their intelligent eyes holding the knowledge for a while. Once seen as omens of ill fortune, their croaks could become cryptic whispers, the main Enoch closer to hidden ability and forgotten pathways. The prospect of Enoch's future was fraught with lurking hazards. The Watchers, twisted reflections in their heavenly selves, could see Enoch suspiciously. They might see his connection to the divine as a hazard, a venture to their waning electricity. Their fallen brethren, demonic entities who thrived in the absence of the divine light, might also be attracted to him, looking to extinguish the glint of hope he carried. But Enoch would not be by myself. Michael, the warrior angel, could watch over him unseen. He would not intervene without delay, but his presence could subtly shift the tides of destiny, nudging occasions in Enoch's want every time the darkness threatened to weigh him down. His journey would not be a straightforward quest for a single artefact. The knowledge he looked for changed into scattered across the land, woven into ancient ruins, cryptic works of art, and forgotten songs sung with the aid of wandering bards. He would have to decipher riddles, triumph over foxy guardians, navigate treacherous landscapes, and even grapple with the developing despair plaguing the sector. But, with each assignment conquered and every layer of knowledge unearthed, Enoch could develop stronger. The forgotten language might appear as part of him, not simply words on a web page, but a dwelling conduit through which he ought to speak with the divine. He might not only effectively wield the energy of the language but also the empathy it fostered, the ability to bridge the gap between humans and the heavenly beings who had once watched over them with benevolence. His adventure would not simply be bridging the gap with the beyond but also about shaping the future. By mending the damaged covenant, he would surely bring the light again; he would usher in a brand-new era of understanding, an international wherein humanity and the divine coexisted in harmony, respecting each other's strength and barriers. The weight of this responsibility pressed closely on Enoch, but the whispers of the angels spurred him on. He was not only a villager anymore; he was an image of wish, a bridge among worlds, and the last chance for a world on the point of falling into oblivion. As he ventured forth, the inscription clutched in his hand, the forgotten phrases resonating inside him, Enoch knew this became the most effective start. His journey, guided by the heavenly realm and fueled by his unwavering religion, would decide the fate of humanity and rewrite the very material of their fact. Enoch's heart raced with excitement and apprehension as he launched into his journey of divine calling. The weight of the Lord's words lingered in his thoughts, a steady reminder of the sacred mission bestowed upon him. With every step he took, he felt a deep experience of purpose guiding him forward, a flicker of willpower that burned brightly within his soul. As he traversed through rugged terrain and luxurious valleys, Enoch found himself experiencing moments of profound reference to the world around him. The splendour of nature opened before his eyes in all its tricky detail, from the colourful shades of a blooming flower to the gentle whispers of the wind through the timber. He felt an experience of kinship with the earth and all its creatures, an attention that each residing being became part of a more complete, deeply connected part of diverse lifestyles. Enoch sought solace in prayer and contemplation in his solitude, looking to deepen his reference to the divine. He spent hours meditating beneath the significant expanse of the starlit sky, his soul reaching out to the heavens in search of steerage and knowledge. And in the quiet moments of reflection, he felt a presence surrounding him. This comforting embrace crammed him with a profound feeling of peace. Enoch's journey persisted as days became weeks and weeks into months, taking him into familiar and unknown lands. Along the way, he met demanding situations and hardships, testing the depths of his faith and resolve. Yet with every obstacle he confronted, Enoch determined strength within the understanding that he became now not by me, that the hand of the divine guided him ever onward. Enoch delved deeper into the mysteries of the universe, his quest for knowledge pushing him to discover the depths of his soul. He contemplated the nature of life, the complexities of destiny and free will, and the interconnectedness of all dwelling matters. The more he learned, the more he found out how little he knew, humbled through the vastness of ability that lay before him. And so, Enoch walked in the direction laid out earlier than him, his spirit ablaze with the fire of divine motive. With unwavering faith and a heart full of devotion, he embraced the mysteries of the universe and the revelations that awaited him on his sacred quest. In that journey of discovery and transformation, Enoch determined not just his authentic calling but also a profound connection with the source of all advent that might forever shape his future.

Chapter 13: A Sacred Encounter

Exhaustion gnawed at Enoch's bones, a relentless wasteland solar having baked the existence out of him for days. Once crisp parchment, the inscription felt limp and damp with sweat in his hand. He had reached the sacred mountain, a solitary peak shrouded in legend and whispers of forgotten knowledge. But doubt, a bitter aftertaste in his mouth, threatened to sour his remedy. Was this a limp surrender, another merciless twist in a seemingly limitless odyssey? As he slumped at the mountain's base, searching for a haven from the relentless solar, the arena dissolved in a dizzying wave. When his vision cleared, he was not on the solar-baked slopes but in a breathtaking vista that confounded description. Cascading waterfalls shimmered with an otherworldly luminescence, their sound a symphony that soothed the raw ache in his muscle mass. Light, a pure, airy type, bathed the panorama in a glow that warmed him to his very middle. And then, he saw Him. A discern of natural electricity stood before him, its significant shape encompassing much of his vision. Yet, notwithstanding its immense length, it radiated warmth and serenity, a palpable feeling that washed over Enoch like a light wave. It became the Holy One, now not a voice from the recesses of his desires, but a being of not possible strength and style. Enoch fell to his knees, beaten by the sheer presence before him. "H-Holy One," he stammered, voice barely a choked whisper. The ground pulsed with a faint vibration as he spoke, a testimony to the outstanding power radiating from the discern. "Is... is that this actual?" The figure smiled, and a wave of soothing strength washed over Enoch. It felt like a balm to his weary soul, easing the tension that had coiled tight in his muscle mass for weeks. "Fear not, Enoch," boomed a voice that resonated within his very being, which became powerful and comforting. "This is a space between realities, an area where we will communicate face-to-face." Enoch regarded it, tears welling in his eyes. This wasn't a dream, a merciless trick. His thoughts became gambling on him inside the throes of exhaustion. This became actual. The weight of the sector, the load of his obligation, pressed down on him with renewed force. "Why me?" he rasped, his voice uncooked with emotion. "Why have you chosen me to hold this burden?" The Holy

One gestured toward the inscription clutched in Enoch's hand. It pulsed with a faint light as though responding to the divine presence. "For within you resides the spark of the covenant, Enoch. You have been born underneath its waning lightness, and it has nurtured inside you the characteristics essential for this mission – compassion, empathy, and unwavering faith in the good of humanity." Shame flooded Enoch. It wasn't the giant demons he'd anticipated, no longer a few outside pressures hell-bent on destruction. The darkness became an outcome, a gaping wound left through humanity's missteps. "We… We strayed, didn't we? We forgot the way to listen, the way to apprehend your ways." The Holy One's voice softened, a light rumble that echoed inside the serene area. "Misunderstandings occur, Enoch. It isn't about blame but finding a route to return to harmony. With the forgotten language resonating inside you, you are the important thing. By unlocking the secrets of the beyond and teaching humanity the language of the covenant, you may reignite the relationship." Enoch's thoughts raced. The inscription, the exhausting journey, it all made me feel now. But the questions persisted in churning inside him. "The darkness... it consumes our vegetation, withers our land. Why does it appear?" "The darkness isn't an entity, Enoch," the Holy One defined, the light emanating from him washing away the shadows that had accrued in Enoch's heart. "It is the absence of light. The fracturing of the covenant has severed the connection between humanity and the divine, the source of light and guidance. Without it, your international is left vulnerable, liable to worry, greed, and melancholy. These, in flip, occur as the darkness you notice plaguing your land." Enoch understood. The darkness wasn't some physical entity to be conquered but a symptom of a deeper illness. Humanity, adrift without the guiding light of the divine, had strayed down a path of destruction. A direction paved with fear, misunderstanding, and a growing disconnect from the very essence of their life. "We can exchange that, can't we?" Enoch dared to invite, a flicker of desire igniting in his chest. The Holy One's voice boomed with energy that despatched shivers down Enoch's spine yet held an underlying warm temperature. "Change is feasible, Enoch, but it will not be easy. You will face challenges and risks to check "...Your remedy and religion. The Watchers, guardians of forgotten expertise, will view you with suspicion. Their electricity wanes with the broken covenant, and they may see your connection to the divine as a chance. Demonic entities, which thrive within the absence of light, could be interested in you, searching to extinguish the flicker of desire you convey." Enoch's heart pounded in opposition to his ribs like a trapped hen. The journey beforehand appeared more daunting than ever, a treacherous route fraught with threat. Images of menacing figures and sizable creatures flashed through his thoughts. Sensing his worry, the Holy One lowered his voice, the booming sound replaced by a gentle hum that vibrated through Enoch's very being. "Fear no longer, Enoch," he reassured, the phrases a balm to his anxieties. "You will not be by yourself. The angels, heavenly beings that watch over humanity, will guide you in subtle approaches. Seraph, the angel of awareness, will seem like ravens, their croaks carrying cryptic messages and leading you to hidden information. Michael, the warrior angel, could be an unseen defence, subtly influencing activities to persuade you clean of immediate peril." Enoch clung to those phrases, a lifeline in a sea of uncertainty. He understood now – his journey wasn't a solitary one. Heavenly forces, unseen but ever-present, could guide his steps and protect him from the worst risks lurking in the shadows. "What about the inscription?" he requested, his voice gaining a newfound strength. "How will it help me bridge the chasm between us and the divine?" The Holy One gestured closer to the parchment, the inscription glowing brighter below his gaze. "The inscription," he defined, "is a fraction of the covenant, a reminder of the language once used to talk with the divine. It is the key to unlocking the forgotten knowledge – understanding to help you most effectively apprehend the inscription's electricity and pave the way for the restoration of the covenant." A thrill of wish coursed through Enoch. The inscription wasn't only a cryptic message; it was a residing piece of their forgotten connection. By deciphering its secrets and techniques and gaining knowledge of the language it held, he could emerge as not just a translator but a bridge – a bridge between the human realm and the heavenly aircraft. "There are tons you may find out, Enoch," the Holy One persevered, his voice resonating with a quiet power.

"You will examine a time whilst humanity and the divine coexisted in harmony, a country of balance that nourished the world and its population. You may also witness the unravelling of the covenant, the misunderstandings that brought about worry and, in the end, the darkness that now consumes your land." Knowledge could be his weapon, both of the past and future. With it, he couldn't only recognize the hassle and formulate a solution. A solution that would not contain violence or conquest but expertise and a rekindled connection. "The path that lies ahead may be lengthy and exhausting, Enoch," the Holy One concluded, the considerable landscape around them starting to shimmer and fade. "But I no longer doubt my faith in you. You had been selected for this venture due to the energy of your spirit and the unwavering flame of empathy that burns inside you. Go forth, Enoch, and with the understanding I have bestowed upon you, be the light that course humanity returned to harmony." The international dissolved another time, and Enoch located himself at the foot of the solar-baked mountain, the inscription clutched tightly in his hand. He became not a weary visitor, misplaced and uncertain of himself. He became a delegated one, a bridge among worlds, a beacon of desire for a global teetering on the threshold. The weight of his responsibility settled closely upon him, but it wasn't a burden. It became a cause, a calling that fueled a hearth within him – the hearth of desire, the fireplace of religion, the hearth that would not be extinguished until humanity and the divine walked hand-in-hand again. With newfound dedication and the promise of the Holy One echoing in his mind, Enoch rose, a changed guy ready to face the demanding situations that lay in advance. His adventure had no longer ended; it had just begun. As the discerning words echoed in the stillness of the evening, Enoch felt a surge of emotions welling up inside him. It became as if a dam had burst open inside his soul, flooding his being with fear, excitement, and a deep feeling of reason. The weight of the divine calling pressed down on him like a heavy mantle, but he knew deep down that he could not pull away from this future that beckoned him onward. The figure earlier than him seemed to shimmer with an otherworldly lightness, its simultaneously familiar and foreign capabilities. Enoch tried to make out its face to understand some semblance of recognition. Still, it remained elusive, as though veiled in a cloak of mystery. And no matter the uncertainty that gripped his heart, Enoch felt an experience of trust and reverence toward this celestial being. This feeling carried expertise far past his very own expertise. "You had been selected for a first-rate motive, Enoch," the discern intoned, its voice resonating with a melodic first-class that seemed to vibrate through the air around them. "The world is in turmoil, misplaced in shadows of doubt and melancholy. But you, my chosen one, preserve inside you a light that may remove darkness from the darkness, a strength that may carry hope and recovery to all trying to find it. Will you take up this mantle of obligation, this burden of greatness, and walk the direction before you?" Enoch's mind raced with 1000 minds, his heart torn between the comfort of his acquainted life and the appeal of the unknown that lay beforehand. But deep within his being, he felt a stirring of fact, a conviction that this became his second hazard to make a difference in a global that so desperately needed it. And so, with a voice filled with determination, he replied, "I receive this calling, anything it may entail. I will heed your divine steering and stroll in this direction with braveness and religion. Lead me, O mysterious one, and I shall comply with any place you may lead." And as Enoch spoke those phrases, a sense of peace washed over him, a reassurance that he was on the right path, guided by forces beyond his comprehension. The discern earlier than him nodded in acknowledgement, its form shimmering earlier than dissolving into a cascade of golden light that enveloped Enoch in a warm embody. And in that moment, because the final rays of daylight faded into the night, Enoch knew that his lifestyle had been forever modified by this sacred come upon, placing him on a route towards a future more than he could have ever imagined. Enoch stood there within the fading light, feeling profound awe and surprise at the importance of what had transpired. The weight of his newfound project settled upon his shoulders like a crown, both a burden and a blessing that he knew he ought to bring with unwavering remedy. As he began to gaze out into the darkening horizon, a sense of motive filled his heart, riding him forward into the unknown with a courage that surprised even himself. He knew that the course beforehand could be fraught with challenges and limitations, but he also knew that he became not on his own. The mysterious figure had entrusted him with a power and a reason that transcended his wildest desires, and he was determined to honour that belief with each fibre of his being. Enoch set forth into the night with a renewed sense of determination, his steps guided by a light that burned brightly inside him, a beacon of hope and redemption in a global that so desperately needed it. As he walked toward his destiny, the celebs above seemed to shine with a new brilliance, as though celebrating the beginning of a hero who might upward thrust to meet the demanding situations of his time and possibly alternate the path of records all the time.

CHAPTER 14: FILLED WITH AWE AND REVERENCE

Enoch blinked away the remnants of the heavenly light as he saw himself standing in a widespread, echoing corridor. Gone became the serene panorama of his assembly with the Holy One; pillars stretched toward an unseen ceiling in its region, their surfaces etched with problematic symbols that pulsed with a faint luminescence. The air hummed with an otherworldly power, an undeniable presence that sent shivers down his spine. A parent materialised from the shadows; its form was cloaked in shimmering white robes that started to soak up the light around it. A light smile graced its youthful face, and its eyes, the colouration of twilight skies, held an ability that belied its younger appearance. "Enoch," the discern boomed, the voice deep and resonant for this slender body. "Welcome to the Temple of Understanding, a reflection of the concord between humanity and the divine." Enoch immediately recognised the being from the whispers in his dreams – Seraph, the angel of awareness. He bowed low, his heart pounding in his chest. "Lady Seraph," he stammered voice barely above a whisper. "It... it's far from an honour." Seraph chuckled, a legitimate wind chime dancing in a light breeze. "Rise, Enoch. You have an awful lot to examine, an awful lot to peer at. Consider this a primer, a glimpse into the records you should apprehend to bridge the chasm between your global and the divine." With a wave of her hand, the symbols on the pillars flickered and morphed, reworking into shifting pictures. Enoch gasped as he saw scenes of an ancient technology unfold earlier than him. Lush landscapes teemed with lifestyles, human beings and heavenly beings coexisting in a country of nonviolent concord. Children played with winged creatures, farmers tended their fields guided through shimmering orbs of light, and elders obtained ability at once from beings of natural electricity. A pang of longing pierced Enoch's heart. This was the arena he became combating to repair, a global in which humanity did not exist in worry of the unknown but in awe of their heavenly companions. Seraph continued the excursion through corridors covered with art depicting the blossoming of knowledge and the forging of the covenant. Each photo, vibrant and exact, etched itself into Enoch's reminiscence. He saw scholars decoding the secrets of the cosmos, architects receiving divine ideas for wondrous structures, and healers mastering faucets into the essence of life itself. But the tour did not just show the wonders of a bygone generation. As they ventured deeper into the temple, the photos grew darker, reflecting the cracks that started to spiderweb throughout the once-pristine covenant. Misunderstandings bloomed, suspicion festered, and the once harmonious change of information became guarded secrets and techniques. Enoch saw a human leader, consumed by ambition, defying the knowledge of a heavenly guide. A tremor ran through the pix, a physical manifestation of the fracturing bond. Harmony gave manners to fear, admiration to suspicion, and communication to isolation. The final picture depicted an international shrouded in darkness, starkly evaluating the colourful scenes from the beginning. Humanity toiled in a barren panorama without the heavenly light that had once nourished them. The silence within the sizable chamber changed into deafening. Enoch stood there, the weight of records urgent down on him. He had seen the consideration, fall, light, and darkness. Now, he understood the importance of his task – to repair the fractured covenant and ensure this type of misunderstanding never retook root. Seraph placed a light hand on his shoulder, a silent reassurance inside the face of his overwhelming burden. "The journey beforehand will be fraught with demanding situations, Enoch," she said, her voice smooth but full of unwavering electricity. "But bear in mind, you are not on my own. The training you have witnessed here is your manual, a reminder of the beyond that can form destiny." Enoch appeared at the angel, a newfound determination burning in his eyes. "I apprehend, Lady Seraph. I will not allow the darkness to win. I will bridge the chasm and repair the light." A faint smile graced the angel's lips. "That is the spirit, Enoch," she declared. Her voice took on a more serious tone. "But bear in mind, the direction to restoring the covenant is not just about learning the forgotten language. It is simply the basis of the reconnection. Humans strayed from the course of humility and respect in their pursuit of knowledge and electricity. They started to see themselves as masters in their world, forgetting their dependence on the divine spark that nurtured existence itself." Enoch contemplated her phrases. He understood now. Restoring the covenant was not a conversation; it became an essential shift in attitude. Humanity had to rediscover its place within the grand scheme of life to recognize the threads by which all that matter is held together. Seraph led him to a smaller chamber, its walls coated with heavenly scrolls. "These "...These scrolls," Seraph persevered, her voice echoing softly inside the chamber, "contain the forgotten knowledge, now not just of the language, but of the philosophy underpinning the covenant. Here, you'll study the heavenly attitude, how the divine considered humanity, and the delicate stability that existed." Enoch's hands grazed the easy surface of a scroll, the difficult script shimmering with an internal light. He felt a surge of pleasure mixed with apprehension. The understanding within these scrolls became important to knowledge, not simply the language but the very essence of the connection that needed mending. "It will now not be clean," Seraph warned, sensing his trepidation. "The heavenly language isn't always simply words, Enoch. It is a language of emotions, empathy, and knowledge of the material truth. It will project your perceptions and force you to peer into the arena through a specific lens." Enoch took a deep breath, his remedy solidifying. He changed into preparing for the mission. With each scroll he deciphered, he would not just be gaining knowledge of a new way to talk; he might be taking a giant soar toward information, the essence of the divine and humanity's place within its grand layout. Seraph smiled, a warmth radiating from her form. "Then let us start," she said, her voice like a gentle breeze. "Let us delve into the forgotten past and, from its ashes, forge a new destiny for your international." As Seraph guided him through the first scroll, unfolding its secrets and nuances, Enoch felt a connection with the heavenly realm that he had experienced before. It was not getting knowledge; it became a profound shift within him. He started to peer into the arena via a double lens — the human perspective he embodied and the heavenly angel he slowly unlocked. Days changed into weeks, weeks into months, as Enoch immersed himself in the heavenly scrolls. He learned of the divine standards governing the universe, the interconnectedness of all matters, and the sensitive stability between the fabric and the non-secular nation-states. He learned of the feelings that flowed through the heavenly language — now not just joy and sorrow, but wisdom, compassion, and a profound appreciation for the complicated dance of life in all its paperwork. With each passing day, Enoch felt a change taking hold. He was not just becoming a translator; he became a bridge, a living embodiment of the covenant he looked for to restore. He understood now that the darkness was not a physical entity to be banished but a symptom of deeper contamination – a disconnect from the divine spark that nurtured lifestyles. Finally, the day arrived when Enoch felt assured of his talents. He had mastered the heavenly language and started to embody the very essence of the covenant – empathy, appreciation, and a deep knowledge of the interconnectedness of all matters. He came to Seraph, a newfound heart burning in his eyes. "I am geared up," he declared, his voice organisation and resoluteness. "I am geared up to stand the demanding situations that lie in advance and restore the light to my world." A radiant smile lit up Seraph's face. "I knew you would be, Enoch," she said. "The international awaits your return, a beacon of hope in times of darkness. Go forth and allow the forgotten language to bridge the chasm between your global and the divine." Enoch stepped out of the heavenly realm, now not just a weary traveller but a delegated one, armed with knowledge and a heart brimming with hope. As he descended again to his world, the weight of his responsibility rested upon him, a burden he now carried no longer with worry but unwavering determination. He changed into the bridge, the bearer of light and the closing danger for a global teetering on the brink of melancholy. The journey before him became fraught with danger, but Enoch knew he was not alone. He carried the knowledge of the beyond, the wisdom of the heavenly realm, and the language that might pave the way for a brighter future – a future where humanity and the divine coexisted over again, not in worry and false impression, but in concord and recognition. In the quiet stillness of the morning, Enoch found himself all over again at the threshold of the wooded area, bathed in the golden light of dawn. The air becomes crisp and packed with the candy songs of birds welcoming the brand-new day. As he stood there, surrounded by the beauty of nature, an experience of reverence washed over him. Enoch closed his eyes and took a deep breath, letting the sparkling air fill his lungs. The sound of the rustling leaves and the distant murmur of a nearby flow seemed to hold a message of peace and quietness. He felt a deep connection to the world around him, as though each tree and blade of grass had changed into part of something more divine. Opening his eyes, Enoch regarded the clear blue sky above, where the sun began its ascent. The colourations of the morning painted a masterpiece across the heavens, igniting an experience of marvel and awe inside him. How could one now not be humbled inside the presence of such majesty? As Enoch continued his walk through the wooded area, each step was regarded to echo with profound gratitude. Gratitude for the splendour of the herbal world, the gifts of life and breath, and the countless blessings that surrounded him. It became a sense that crammed his heart to the brim, overflowing with an overwhelming experience of appreciation for all that he had been given. Enoch whispered a silent prayer of way to the Creator, feeling a deep connection to the divine presence that permeated every woodland nook. At that moment, he understood that reference had changed into a feeling and a manner of being in the international community. It became a popularity of the sacredness of all lifestyles, a gratitude for the interconnectedness of all matters. And so, as Enoch walked on, his heart complete and his spirit lifted, he felt awe and reverence that might guide him on his adventure closer to extra knowledge and ability. The forest, with its ancient timber and whispering winds, is regarded to be a residing, breathing entity, encompassing a wisdom far deeper than any phrase may want to carry. Each rustling leaf, each chirping fowl, and every beam of daylight shining past the covering held a message—a message of concord, of balance, of the everlasting dance of existence and loss of life. Enoch felt a sense of belonging, a sense of being a part of something tremendous and timeless. The fragrant earth below his toes, the cool breeze on his skin, and the symphony of nature's voices enveloped him in a cocoon of peace. It changed into these moments, surrounded by the beauty and majesty of the herbal global, that Enoch found solace and renewal. The wooded area became not simply a place of trees and natural world—it changed into a sanctuary, a temple wherein he should commune with the sacred essence that dwelled inside and around him. And so, with every step he took, Enoch delved deeper into the mysteries of life, searching to get to the bottom of the mysteries of the universe and his soul. The woodland whispered its secrets and techniques to him, ancient wisdom passed down for a while, ready to be discovered by using people with eyes to see and ears to hear. And as Enoch walked on, his heart beating coordinated with the heartbeat of the woodland, he knew that he was on a journey of profound importance—an adventure towards enlightenment in the direction of harmony with the divine. Enoch's footsteps, guided by unseen pressure, lead him deeper into the forest's heart. As he ventured in addition, the air around him grew thick with the heady scent of earth and moss, permeated with the energy of the historical bushes that stood sentinel of their silent awareness. The canopy above filtered the daylight into a light golden hue, casting dappled styles on the wooded area floor like a sacred mosaic. With each breath, Enoch felt a sense of peace settle deep within his soul as if the very essence of the woodland were infusing him with its tranquillity. He reached out, touching the tough bark of a towering Oaktree. He felt a pulse of power below his fingertips, a connection to the existing force that thrummed through each living element within the woodland. The symphony of nature's sounds surrounded him, a refrain of chook songs, rustling leaves, and the light babble of a nearby stream. It changed as though the forest itself became alive, speaking to him in a language older than words, whispering secrets and techniques of the earth and the sky, of delivery and loss of life, of cycles eternal and unchanging. Enoch's heart swelled with a gratitude that transcended mere phrases. He became humbled with the aid of the vastness of the natural international, by the difficult web of existence that interconnected all living beings. At this moment, he understood that he was not becoming independent from the woodland but a part of it. As the solar climbed higher inside the sky, bathing the forest in a heat, golden light, Enoch knew that he had seen a sacred place, a sanctuary wherein he may want to come to discover peace and proposal, where he may want to commune with the divine presence that dwelled within and around him. And so, with a heart full of reverence and a spirit lifted by the beauty of the wooded area, he continued his adventure, guided by the historical knowledge that resonated in the heart of the natural world. Enoch stood inside the presence of the divine being, feeling an experience of overwhelming reverence and awe. The entity before him emanated a heavenly light that bathed the chamber in a golden glow, casting tricky patterns on the stone partitions. Enoch's heart raced with fear and pleasure as he gazed upon the being's radiant form. The voice that resonated from the being changed into like a symphony of the heavens, every phrase sporting the load of eternity. It referred to a grand cosmic plan, a destiny intertwined with the very cloth of introduction. Enoch felt a deep connection to the being, as though he had recognised it for an eternity as if it held the key to his real reason for existing on this earth. The message spread out elaborately before Enoch like a sea of divine understanding, each wave flooded with a story of redemption and transformation. It mentioned trials and tribulations, of sacrifices that must be made to satisfy the sacred challenge beforehand. Enoch's heart swelled with a combination of trepidation and resolution as he absorbed the size of the challenge. As the being's words continued flowing, Enoch felt an experience of readability washing over him, a profound understanding of his place within the plane of human and heavenly existence. He knew that he became known for a better purpose, that his actions could ripple through the cosmos and leave an indelible mark on the sector. The being mentioned was a first-rate cosmic battle, a conflict between light and darkness that had raged for aeons. Enoch's role in this warfare was to be a beacon of hope, a warrior for the forces of truth in an international teetering on the threshold of chaos. The being discovered to him historic prophecies and forgotten truths, unlocking energy within him that he had by no means acknowledged existed. With a deep breath, Enoch raised his head and met the gaze of the divine being. He may want to sense the load of its gaze upon him, a silent acknowledgement of the solemn vow he was about to adopt. At that moment, Enoch knew his existence would not be the same, that he had changed into someone destined for greatness past his wildest goals. Determined and resolute, Enoch took a breakthrough, geared up to embrace the divine project bestowed upon him. The being's presence surrounded him like a cloak of heavenly lightness, guiding his every step as he embarked on the adventure that would shape his destiny and the destiny of all who dwelled inside the universe.

CHAPTER 15: A JOURNEY OF GRATITUDE

Enoch stood at the brink between realities, the heavenly air shimmering around him like the mark of a majestic presence. He moved closer to Seraph, her angelic form radiating warm temperature and light encouragement. Months, or even years, had surpassed this realm of pure energy, time losing its grip amidst the whirlwind of ability he had absorbed. Gratitude, a deep and abiding feeling, filled him. He bowed low, his head brushing the airy floor. "Thank you, Lady Seraph," he said, his voice packed with emotion. "For your endurance, steerage, and beginning my eyes to the forgotten information." Seraph chuckled, a legitimate wind chime dancing within the twilight.

"There is no want for such formalities, Enoch. You have discovered a good deal, and you have grown even more. The knowledge you bring isn't always mine to thank me for, but yours – an earned treasure to carry lower back for your international." Enoch appeared across the fantastic temple one last time, his gaze lingering on the heavenly scrolls that had unlocked the secrets and techniques of the past. He was not simply living with knowledge; he began living with a converted heart, a lens through which he could see the sector anew. Now imbued with deeper knowledge, the inscription pulsed faintly in his hand, a steady reminder of his assignment. A faint breeze stirred, sporting the whispers of the coming adventure. A pang of apprehension flickered inside him, fast changed by using a surge of dedication. Though the direction ahead would not be easy, he was not the same man who had first stumbled through the desert sands, searching for solutions. He was Enoch, the bridge between worlds, armed with the forgotten language and a burning desire to repair the light of his international. He came again to Seraph, a newfound fireplace blazing in his eyes. "I understand the challenges that look ahead to me," he declared, his voice organisation and resoluteness. "But I also understand the hope in the forgotten language, a desire for knowledge and a brighter destiny." Seraph smiled, the wrinkles around her eyes deepening. "And it's a hope you should hold dear, Enoch," she said, "so it will carve your way through the darkness. Remember, the language is not simply phrases to be spoken but a bridge of empathy and providing knowledge. Use it accurately, and it can mend the fractured covenant and usher in a brand-new generation of harmony." With a very last bow of gratitude, Enoch improved. The warm temperature of his personal truth enveloped him, the heavenly light giving way to the harsh glare of the wasteland solar. He blinked, the stark panorama momentarily blurring earlier than entering focus. The inscription, warm in his hand, felt like a familiar friend, symbolising all he had learned and the load he now carried with pride. He appeared toward the remote horizon, his heart swelling with a newfound motive. The journey back would be long and exhausting, filled with perils and uncertainties. But Enoch now did not confront them alone. He carried the electricity of the forgotten language, the knowledge of the heavenly realm, and the unwavering promise of a brighter destiny. He became ready. He became the bridge, and he went home. Enoch brings them healing and deliverance from the misplaced phrase as he passes through cities, and they are very thankful. The relentless desolate solar tract beat down on Enoch as he trudged through the dunes, the inscription clutched tightly in his hand. He was not simply traversing a bodily landscape; he became on a healing pilgrimage, carrying the forgotten language like a flickering torch in the darkness. The first city he met became a lonely photo of despair. Crops withered within the fields, the once energetic rectangular market lay eerily silent, and a palpable fear hung heavy in the air. Whispers painted a grim photo – an unusual blight had ravaged their lands, accompanied by illness and a chilling silence from the gods they once respected. Enoch approached the town elder, a wizened guy with fear etched on his face. As he spoke the forgotten language, his voice resonated with odd electricity, sporting not simply phrases but an outpouring of empathy for their plight. To begin with, the elder, Wary, felt a wave of understanding wash over him. Enoch referred to the imbalance caused by humanity's forgotten connection to the divine. Together, they deciphered the inscription, a file of forgotten rituals celebrating the bond between humanity and the earth. Enoch guided the townspeople as they finished the rituals, talking the lost phrases with newfound appreciation. As they chanted, light rain fell, the first in months. The parched earth drank it greedily, and the entire city heaved a sigh of relief. Once a cryptic puzzle, the inscription started to glow faintly, a subtle acknowledgement of the renewed connection it had helped foster. News of Enoch's arrival and the unbelievable rain unfolded like wildfire. The city he visited later became plagued by a special kind of darkness. Here, worry had morphed into suspicion and violence. Accusations flew as plants inexplicably withered, and a paranoid mob held the village healer captive, blaming him for the misfortune. Enoch stepped into the chaos, his presence radiating calm. He spoke now to the villagers and the healer held captive; his phrases were imbued with relaxing information. He discovered how the damaged covenant had weakened their connection to the divine, making them prone to the whispers of the Watchers, fallen guardians who thrived on discord. As Enoch spoke, the healer's eyes widened in recognition. He testified to the dark whispers that had fueled his anxieties and suspicions. The villagers, surprised, diminished their guns. A shared obligation settled upon them – to rebuild the covenant and mend the bridge between humanity and the divine. Enoch's adventure was not a chain of short fixes. Each settlement he reached offered a unique assignment, a symptom of the fractured bond. He confronted distrustful nomads who had deserted their ancestral lands, convinced the divine had cursed them. He met desolate villages ravaged by dust storms, a consequence of humanity's brush aside for the delicate balance of the herbal world. He even came throughout communities ravaged with the aid of sickness, in which fear and despair had curdled right into a self-pleasing prophecy. He tackled those challenges not with a single solution but with the forgotten language, his voice appearing as a bridge, forging understanding and fostering empathy. With the nomads, they spoke of the significance of harmony with the land, revealing forgotten rituals that soothed the earth and ensured its persevering bounty. In the dirt-choked villages, he guided human beings in rituals of admiration for the winds and the elements, reminding them of the interconnected fabric of lifestyles. He said faith and resilience for the ill communities, channelling the forgotten language into a symphony of desire and luxury that strengthened their spirits and spurred them to seek forgotten herbal remedies. With every metropolis he visited, the inscription grew brighter, the lost language resonating deeper within him. It was no longer words on parchment;

it became a living essence laden with respect, humility, and a shared responsibility for their inhabited sector. He was not only a translator; he became a testimony to the forgotten energy of communication, of empathy bridging the chasm between the human and the divine. As whispers of "The Bridge Walker' and "The Voice of the Forgotten' spread across the land, a ripple of anguish started to spread in the darkness. Enoch's journey was not a race to a finish line; it became a marathon of knowledge. He learned now not just about the forgotten language but the depths of human resilience and the insidious methods depression may want to appear. Each town and assignment chipped away at the darkness, now not with a dramatic flourish but with the quiet, continual light of rediscovery. The road ahead remained long, a large and desolate panorama shrouded within the remnants of humanity's errors. But with each leap forward and every network he touched, the memory of a harmonious past flickered brighter, and the future he strived for, a destiny in which humanity and the divine coexisted in light and knowledge, felt a touch nearer. The inscription, now a beacon shimmering in his hand, was a consistent reminder of his reason – to grow to be the bridge that could someday lead his "...Human beings back into the warm include of the divine."

Days bled into weeks, and the relentless solar was a consistent partner. Yet, a growing hearth in his spirit countered the fatigue that gnawed at Enoch's frame. The whispers of wish he had ignited in each town fueled his remedy, a refrain that grew louder with each step he took. His journey culminated at the foot of a significant mountain variety, its peaks shrouded in swirling mist. Legend noted a hidden metropolis nestled inside, a town once teeming with communique between humans and the heavenly beings. It was right here, the whispers recommended, that the final key to restoring the covenant lay hidden. The ascent became exhausting, the air growing skinny and the direction treacherous. Yet,

Enoch pressed on, the forgotten language a mantra on his lips. He confronted blizzards that howled like banshees and navigated rocky cliffs that tested his balance. But for each project, he overcame, the reminiscence of a revitalised town and the faces of human beings reconnected to the light spurred him onward. Finally, after days of relentless hiking, he reached a hidden plateau shrouded in a veil of mist. As he stepped forward, the mist dissipated, revealing a panoramic vista. Sprawled before him lay a remarkable, deserted town, its architecture a testimony to an ancient technology of harmony. He had reached the fabled town of Elyon. As he entered the town, an experience of overwhelming disappointment washed over him. Magnificent structures stood empty, monuments to a misplaced connection. Here, wherein communique flourished, now the best silence echoed. He wandered into libraries full of forgotten scrolls, their secrets waiting to be rediscovered. He reached a crucial plaza, its layout resonating with a heavenly design he found during his time with Seraph. A monolithic obelisk stood at the plaza's heart, pulsating with celestial power. Enoch instinctively knew this was the key he was looking for. He approached it, the inscription in his hand sparkling brighter with each step. As he reached out to touch the obelisk, a voice boomed within his mind, resonating with electricity and laced with a hint of sorrow. "Enoch," the voice echoed, "you have an extended manner. But the route in advance is the most critical." Enoch diagnosed the voice – the Holy One. He knelt, his heart pounding in his chest. He said his voice corporation was geared up despite the awe threatening to crush him. "The inscription," the Holy One endured, "holds the important thing to restoring the covenant, but it calls for a sacrifice – a bridge now not just of verbal exchange, but of revelling in. Are you inclined to bear that burden, Enoch?" Enoch understood. Restoring the covenant was not about phrases but about living the message, embodying the forgotten bond between humanity and the divine. He did not hesitate. "I am," he declared, his voice ringing clear. A light wave engulfed him, bathing him in a heavenly warm temperature. When it subsided, the inscription in his hand had vanished, changed with the aid of a faint heavenly mark etched on his forehead. The mark pulsed with a smooth luminescence, a steady reminder of the duty he now bore. He looked again at the obelisk. Words, etched in heavenly and human language, shimmered into life. It was a very last message from the Holy One, a guide for the final leg of his journey: "Speak now not just with words, Enoch, but together with your actions. Be the bridge, and manual your humans returned to the light." Enoch stood tall, his heart brimming with motivation. He had traversed the physical landscape, faced endless demanding situations, and even bridged the gap between worlds. Now, the most important part of his adventure started: guiding humanity lower back to the light, one action, one phrase, one shared understanding at a time. He went far from the amazing town, the setting sun painting the sky in colours of desire. His adventure as a translator is over, but his adventure as the bridge, the embodiment of the covenant, has started. And as he walked down the mountain, the mark on his brow sparkling faintly, Enoch knew he would not be strolling alone. The echoes of his voice imbued with the forgotten language and the power of ability, would keep rippling throughout the land, igniting a spark of wish that could, in the end, engulf the sector and bring in an innovative technology of harmony. Enoch's footsteps echoed softly across the ancient woodland, his heart a tumultuous blend of emotions as he navigated the dimly lit direction before him. The dense cover overhead filtered the fading light of day, casting dappled shadows that danced like spectres along the moss-blanket ground. The whispered secrets and techniques of the ancient bushes were about to develop louder, their voices blending into the murmuring chorus surrounding him. As he walked, Enoch could not shake the feeling of being watched, of unseen eyes following his every flow with a combination of curiosity and apprehension. It became as though the very spirits of the forest were roused by his presence, stirring from their slumber to witness the unfolding occasions that had led him to this sacred region. His mind drifted back to the instant of revelation, the divine message that had seared into his awareness like a brand. The weight of the assignment pressed heavily upon his shoulders in advance, a burden that threatened to weigh down his spirit with its sheer enormity. Yet, no matter the doubt that gnawed at the rims of his resolve, Enoch saw solace within the memories of the blessings that had fashioned his journey so far. The laughter of loved ones, the embrace of a starlit sky, the warm temperature of a kind word spoken in moments of darkness—all whispered of a lifestyle lived in concord with the rhythms of the universe. And in that harmony, Enoch found strength, a wellspring of courage that flowed from the depths of his soul like a river replenished through the eternal waters of religion. As the forest grew darker and the celebs above sparkled like diamonds in the velvet sky, Enoch felt a profound connection to the unseen forces that guided his steps. The air started to thrum with palpable electricity, a symphony of whispers and rustling leaves that pointed out a world past the rims of mortal belief. And in that second of communion with the divine, Enoch knew that he became not on my own in his quest. Gathering his remedy, he set his jaw. He squared his shoulders, ready to face the challenges ahead with a heart steeped in gratitude and a spirit fortified by faith. The shadows of the wooded area did not hold sway over him, for he walked with the knowledge that his journey was now not considered one of solitude but of sacred companionship with the unseen hands that guided his fate. And as he ventured deeper into the heart of the forest, his steps filled with motive and his heart alight with the heart of divine revelation, Enoch knew that he became sure of a future that transcended the confines of mortal knowledge.

CHAPTER 16: EMBRACING THE SACRED PURPOSE

As Enoch journeyed deeper into the heartland, the whispers that preceded him evolved from curiosity to determined pleas. News of the "Bridge Walker" and the "Voice of the Forgotten" had morphed into a more potent moniker – "The One Who Saves." People flocked to him, their eyes brimming with desperation and a glimmer of wish that glinted like a candle inside the wind. The weight of this title settled closely on Enoch's shoulders. He was not a superhero descending from the heavens, nor did he become a charismatic chief promising on-the-spot salvation. He became a man, a scholar pressured with the forgotten language, a bridge between fractured humanity and the divine. The first encounter that certainly rattled Enoch became a village decimated by using a virulent disease. As he approached, a gaunt female threw herself at his feet, sobbing. "Save us, blessed one!" she cried, her voice uncooked with despair. "You are our best wishes!" Enoch, familiar with sceptical glances and wary welcomes, became stunned. He knelt earlier than the female, his voice gentle. "I can't treat the plague," he said without a doubt, "but I can help you apprehend the reasons behind it, the imbalance that brought this struggling." The woman appeared momentarily deflated, but a flicker of knowledge remained in her eyes. He spoke to them about the forgotten rituals of respect for nature and the interconnectedness of all matters. As the villagers listened, an experience of community and purpose bloomed around him. They were not looking for a miracle remedy but a way to heal themselves and their land. While the villagers were not awaiting a miracle, others did. In the next city, a charismatic leader, facing a revolt fueled by hunger, hailed Enoch as the answer to their woes. "He speaks the language of the gods!" the leader declared, inciting the gang. "He will convey us rain and bountiful harvests!" Enoch saw himself swept up in a political whirlwind, his message twisted to serve the leader's schedule. He tried to propose and explain that the answer lay in knowledge, no longer divine intervention. But his words were drowned out with the aid of the cheers of the determined crowd. Disheartened, he retreated to a quiet nook, the burden of the title "The One Who Saves" pressing down on him like a bodily burden. He was not a miracle worker, now not a conquering hero. He changed into a bridge, a translator, a humble guy armed with the forgotten language. That night, underneath the sizable expanse of the star-dusted sky, Enoch confided in his doubts with Seraph, who appeared in a shimmering dream. "They are trying to find a new solution, Enoch," she said, her voice tender yet filled with information. "But the direction to restoring the covenant isn't an act of magic or even miracles. It's about teaching them to understand the language of the universe, the language of respect and communal unity." Enoch clung to her words. He would not shrink back from his function but would not be manipulated. From then on, he faced each town with renewed clarity. He would not promise salvation; he could offer information. He no longer spoke simply as a translator but as a facilitator, supporting groups to rediscover forgotten knowledge and empower themselves to heal their land and mend their connection with the divine. Instead of pronouncing from a pedestal, Enoch's method has affected people's communication. He delved into the forgotten scrolls, deciphering no longer simply words but also the underlying philosophy that once ruled the harmonious courting between humanity and the heavenly realm. He shared this knowledge with the townsfolk, encouraging them to rediscover their own experience of employer and duty. The consequences were not usually immediate or dramatic. In some cities, the seeds of knowledge he sowed took root slowly, blossoming into a sluggish angle shift. In others, the effect became more tangible. For instance, a network plagued by dust storms rediscovered forgotten rituals of appeasing the winds, resulting in calmer skies and renewed boom. The identity "The One

Who Saves" began to take on a new meaning with each step. Enoch was not a unique saviour swooping in to restore the entirety. He became a catalyst, an igniter of forgotten information. He empowered humans to keep to themselves and rebuild their connection with the divine not through blind religion but through a newfound knowledge of the language that bound all of them. The road ahead became long and exhausting, a vast and desolate landscape shrouded within the remnants of humanity's errors. But with his newfound readability and the forgotten language resonating within him, Enoch continued his journey, a beacon of wish in a world teetering on the brink. He became the bridge walker, the voice of the forgotten, and now, the embodiment of a one-of-a-kind sort of salvation – a salvation constructed on knowledge, empathy, and the collective will of a people yearning to reconnect with the light they had forgotten. The whispers had morphed into a chorus. News of "The One Who Saves" travelled faster than the barren region winds, portraying Enoch in a comforting and unnerving light. He became an image of hope, a residing legend whispered in hushed tones around flickering campfires and bustling marketplaces. Yet, with each metropolis he visited, the load of the title grew heavier. A determined populace awaited him in a bustling metropolis-state ruled by an iron fist. They saw him as their simplest hazard to overthrow the tyrant queen. Once he arrived, a mob of residents crowded him, their chants echoing through the streets. "Save us, Enoch! Deliver us from tyranny!" Enoch raised his arms for silence, his heart sinking. He was not a warrior, and violence was not the language of the covenant. He spoke to them of forgotten legal guidelines, of a time when rulers governed with admiration for the divine and for their human beings. He talked about the significance of a simple chief, one that guided as opposed to rule with an iron fist. His phrases resonated with a young scholar, a firebrand imprisoned for dissent. Inspired by Enoch's message, the pupil ignited a rise – now not of bloodshed, but of thoughts. Through clandestine pamphlets and passionate speeches, he fueled a movement that championed the forgotten legal guidelines. The queen, facing a tide of dissent based on the ideas of the covenant itself, noticed the writing on the wall. She surrendered, paving the way for a simpler and fairer rule. Enoch did not overthrow the queen, but his words empowered others to do that. He was not the narrative's hero but the exchange catalyst. This awareness, while beginning with deflating, step by step, settled into a quiet satisfaction. Now, he understood the authentic strength of the forgotten language – no longer as a device for miracles but as a seed of understanding that would blossom into a revolution of perspective. His adventure took him to a desolate wilderness, a once-fertile land ravaged by greed and brushed aside for the herbal world. The people here considered him with suspicion, their desire long extinguished. The forgotten language was not simply words but a name to action. Enoch led them in rediscovering rituals of recognition for the earth, teaching them to apprehend the interconnectedness of people and nature. They rebuilt irrigation systems, planted drought-resistant plants, and fostered a renewed reverence for the land. Slowly, the barren landscape started to expose signs and symptoms of existence. A hesitant blade of inexperience emerged from the cracked earth, a delicate image of wish. This was not dramatic in a single-day transformation but a testimony to the strength of collective action fueled by information. The people right here did not need a unique saviour; they wished for a guide, and Enoch, using the forgotten language, presented a course toward a sustainable future. As he continued his journey, the burden of the name "The One Who Saves" started to change. It did not symbolise a novel, extraordinary saviour, but a collective motion sparked through his actions. He was not simply the bridge; he became the torchbearer, illuminating the forgotten route lower back to the divine. One evening, a vintage woman approached him as he sat by a crackling campfire. Her eyes, though wrinkled with age, held a spark of knowledge. "You are not 'The One Who Saves,'" she said, her voice husky but company. "You are the reminder." Enoch looked at her, a flicker of knowledge dawning in his eyes. He was not the saviour humanity yearned for, a wish-granting genie descending from the heavens. He was the reminder of a forgotten connection, a voice echoing from a bygone era of harmony. He becomes a catalyst, igniting the dormant embers of ability in the hearts of his human beings. The journey in advance remained lengthy and arduous, filled with challenges and setbacks. But Enoch confronted them now not with the burden of a saviour but with the unwavering cause of a reminder. He embodied the forgotten language, not with pronouncements, but with moves. He walked many people, sharing knowledge, fostering empathy, and encouraging their business enterprise. He became the bridge walker, the voice of the forgotten, and now, the reminder – a testimony to the collective strength of understanding that would someday lead humanity to return to the light. Disappointment gnawed at Enoch as he traversed the solar-baked plains. He had expected himself to be a key determiner, a hero wielding the forgotten language to dismantle the darkness shrouding his international. But reality proved to be some distance much less glamorous. He was met with scepticism in the primary village, disregarded as a madman babbling about misplaced tongues. In the second, a charismatic chief twisted his words into pronouncements of divine desire, furthering his very own schedule. Desolation settled over him like the dust swirling throughout the barren landscape. Was this all his adventure becoming destined to be – a sequence of misunderstandings and manipulations? Doubt gnawed at his clear-up, whispering that the forgotten language had changed into only a forgotten relic, its energy long gone. That night, under the beauty of a dark sky lit by stars, Enoch sought solace in a secluded grove. Tears welled up in his eyes, blurring the acquainted inscription on his hand. He seemed up on the heavenly expanse, a silent plea escaping his lips. "What am I supposed to do?" he choked out, his voice ragged. A gentle breeze rustled the leaves, and a luminescent orb materialised above him. It becomes Seraph, her shape shimmering with an airy light. "Enoch," her voice resonated with a relaxing warmth. "Do not despair now. The route you walk is not supposed to be a grand spectacle but a quiet revolution." Enoch checked her out, a flicker of hope rekindling in his heart. "But they do not recognize," he said, his voice thick with frustration. "They twist my words, see me as something I'm no longer..." Seraph smiled a gesture that crinkled the corners of her youthful face. "You are not a miracle worker, Enoch," she said. "You are a bridge, a facilitator of information. The light you carry is not blinding brilliance, but a gentle spark that ignites forgotten knowledge within them." Her words resonated with an unexpected readability. He was not there to dictate answers but to empower. The forgotten language was not a device for instant gratification but a seed that, whilst nurtured, ought to blossom right into a collective shift in angle. A renewed sense of purpose and clarity settled upon him the next morning. He arrived at a village plagued with discord, its people living in worry and suspicion. He did not try grand pronouncements; rather, he focused on forgotten rituals of community and empathy. He spoke in easy terms, translating not just phrases but feelings – admiration, ability, the shared responsibility for their nice being. He noticed a flicker of popularity in their eyes as they rediscovered those forgotten traditions. Slowly, the whispers of fear subsided, replaced with hesitant speech. The villagers started out working together, rebuilding as they rebuilt their lives. There have been no instantaneous miracles, no dramatic differences, just the quiet hum of information starting to resonate through the community. As Enoch persevered in his adventure, he embraced this quiet electricity. He was not just a translator; he became an instructor, a notion. He shared his knowledge with pupils, sparking a motion primarily based on rediscovering forgotten ideas. He spoke to everyday people, farmers, and traders, planting seeds of understanding that manifested in easy acts of respect for the land and their fellow people. His journey was not mere folklore or even about heroic fulfilment. Still, it was a collection of infinite small victories strung together like sparkling beads on a long necklace. He saw villages mending fractured relationships with long-forgotten rituals. He noticed groups embracing sustainable practices after deciphering ancient texts about the earth's sensitive balance. He became a catalyst, a spark that ignited an alternate now, not through pressure, but with the quiet energy of shared knowledge. One night, a younger female approached him as he sat by using a campfire with a group of nomads. Her eyes, vibrant with interest, held not one of the preliminary scepticisms he had met. "You are Enoch, the Bridge Walker," she said, her voice full of awe. Enoch smiled, a warm temperature spreading through him. He was not "The One Who Saves." He becomes the reminder – a reminder of a forgotten connection, a voice echoing from the beyond to illuminate a path to a brighter destiny. He no longer saw sadness in his adventure but a quiet purpose, an obligation he embraced with newfound clarity. He became the bridge walker, the voice of the forgotten, and now, the reminder - a testimony to the strength of understanding and knowledge, the quiet energy that might someday lead humanity again to the light. Enoch stood at the cliff's edge, the wind whipping through his hair and the sound of speeding water from the valley filling his ears. The weight of his newfound reason settled heavily on his shoulders. Still, there was also an experience of peace that followed it. He was chosen for a reason, and he knew he needed to embody this sacred cause with all his heart. The message he had obtained from the divine being had filled him with a feeling of responsibility and importance and an overwhelming feeling of gratitude. As he looked out at the sector unfolding before him, he knew that he had changed his mind and intended to play a good-sized position within the unfolding of activities. He was given a present of connection to the divine, and he understood that this connection got here with a responsibility to use it wisely. Enoch's mind drifted to the historic prophecies that noted a time of first-rate change and upheaval of a designated person who would upward thrust to deliver stability and renewal to a fractured world. Could it be that he became the success of these prophecies, only destined to result in a new age of concord and understanding? With a deep sense of awe and humility, Enoch discovered the size of the assignment that lay before him. It was not just about his journey of self-discovery and increase but about the impact he could have on the lives of others and the material existence itself. As he felt the presence of the divine surrounding him, Enoch knew he was now not by me in his quest. The forces of proper and light stood with him, guiding his steps and offering him strength and information in times of need. Taking a final deep breath, Enoch steeled himself for the demanding situations that lay beforehand. The path before him became shrouded in uncertainty, but he became full of a newfound experience of purpose and resolution. With every step he took, he drew towards his future, geared up to embrace the sacred function bestowed upon him. The sun began to dip underneath the horizon, casting a golden hue over the land. Enoch closed his eyes and allowed himself to bask in the heat glow, feeling an experience of connection to the historical forces that ruled the universe. In that moment of stillness, a vision flashed before his eyes – an imaginative and prescient of a world unfastened from struggling and strife, an international one wherein all beings lived in concord and peace. It changed into a vision of the future he knew he was destined to be in. Opening his eyes, Enoch felt a surge of determination and motive pulsing through his veins. He knew that the adventure in advance might be lengthy and hard, packed with challenges and limitations. Still, he also knew that he did not become by himself. With a heart complete of braveness and a mind as sharp as a blade, Enoch took his first step toward his destiny, towards the fulfilment of the historic prophecies that had foretold of a chosen one who could carry light to a darkened globe. And as he walked into the unknown, he did so with the knowledge that he carried within him the hopes and desires of all who had come earlier than him and could come after.

Chapter 17: The Weight of Responsibility

Moonlight solid an airy glow on the crumbling stone archway, the ultimate remnant of a once-grand bridge spanning a yawning chasm. Enoch stood earlier than it, the forgotten inscription heat against his hand, a stark assessment of the chilling wind that whistled through the ruins. Here, nestled deep within a forgotten library, he had spent weeks deciphering the cryptic symbols, eventually unlocking their meanings. It was not simply knowledge about the heavenly language; it became a prophecy, a revelation that sent a tremor through his very being. The inscription pointed out a harbinger, a bridge walker selected to mend the fractured covenant between humanity and the divine. It talked about a time of despair, where darkness could shroud the land, and a single voice, imbued with the forgotten language, might be humanity's final hope. Enoch stared at the inscription, a chilly dread slithering down his backbone. He was not just a pupil looking for lost knowledge; he became the precursor, the bridge walker. The weight of this revelation slammed into him with the pressure of a collapsing megastar. This was not simply academic curiosity; it had become a quest to salvage the destiny of his world. Doubt gnawed at him. Was he worthy of this mantle? He became a man of words and scrolls, now not a hero cast inside the fires of warfare. He envisioned grand pronouncements, a rallying cry that might unite the fractured world. But the inscription presented no grandeur; it said a quiet revolution, a recovery fuelled with information, no longer pressure. Days bled into weeks as he wrestled along with his newfound ability. He puzzled Seraph, his heavenly guide, his voice laced with trepidation. "The burden feels too tremendous," he confessed, staring out on the desolate panorama from the heavenly realm. Seraph smiled, her eyes radiating warm temperature. "The burden is not yours alone, Enoch," she said. "You are a conduit, a bridge for the forgotten language to glide back into the world. Imagine not a single spark but one thousand embers igniting in receptive hearts." Her phrases struck a chord within him. He would not be a lone wolf fighting a solitary struggle. He will be the spark that ignited the embers of forgotten awareness within humans. The forgotten language was not just words; it became a philosophy, a way of existence that fostered recognition of the divine and the sensitive balance of the sector. Leaving the heavenly realm behind, Enoch felt a renewed course through him. He was not only a translator; he changed into a shepherd, guiding lost sheep back to a forgotten pasture. As he ventured out into the world, he noticed the devastation, the melancholy etched on the faces of ladies and men. But he also noticed a glimmer of desire, a yearning for something better. Every town he visited has become a stepping stone to a grander adventure. He spoke now not just to scholars but to farmers and traders, his voice resonating with quiet authority. He shared memories and rituals, revealing a depth of knowledge transcending mere phrases. He noticed a glimmer of reputation in their eyes as they rediscovered their forgotten connection to the heavenly realm. Gradually, a motion began to take shape, natural and vast. Farmers, stimulated with the aid of forgotten texts, followed sustainable practices that nurtured the land. Artisans, guided by heavenly designs, crafted gadgets that resonated with a forgotten concord. Communities, united by historical rituals, rebuilt and accepted as true with and cooperation. The internationals were not changing in a single day. There were setbacks, a wallet of resistance clinging to the darkness. But Enoch's seeds of understanding had been taking root, blossoming into a collective awakening. He saw the forgotten language now not just spoken but lived, its principles woven into the material of everyday existence. Standing on a hilltop one night, surveying the huge expanse earlier than him, Enoch eventually grasped the proper value of what he had been called into. He was not an unmarried hero; he was the catalyst, the spark that ignited a revolution of ability. He was not simply the bridge walker; he became the bridge itself, a testimony to the electricity of knowledge and the resilience of the human spirit. The adventure in advance becomes lengthy, the course fraught with uncertainties. Still, Enoch walked it with newfound self-assurance, the inscription heat on his hand, a constant reminder of his purpose – to be the bridge, the shepherd, the harbinger of a destiny bathed within the light of a restored covenant. Moonlight streamed into the dusty library window, illuminating the historic scroll clutched in Enoch's trembling hands. The forgotten language, once a source of fascination, now loomed before him like a cryptic prophecy. As he deciphered the final strains, a cold dread settled in his intestine, solidifying into a leaden weight in his chest. The inscription spoke not simply of a forgotten tongue but of a huge challenge – to fix the fractured covenant between humanity and the divine. It talked about a precursor, a bridge walker, chosen to herald a brand-new technology.

The phrases echoed in his mind, chilling attention dawning on him – he, Enoch, the pupil, the translator, was that bridge walker. Panic clawed at his throat. He was not a warrior, a leader of men. He became a man of quiet contemplation, content material inside the dusty embody of historical scrolls. The inscription referred to a darkness shrouding the land, a global teetering on the edge. The weight of this duty, of being humanity's ultimate desire, felt like a crushing blow. Self-doubt, a serpent he thought lengthily vanquished, reared its unsightly head. Was he worthy of this mantle? He expected grand pronouncements, a rallying cry that might unite the fractured international. But the inscription presented no such hero's journey; it saw a diffused shift, a recovery fueled by understanding, now not force. The days were replaced with sleepless nights. The forgotten language, once a source of intellectual curiosity, now felt like a burden, a key to a door he was unsure he was courageous enough to open. He sought solace within the heavenly realm, his voice laced with melancholy as he confided in Seraph. "The challenge is too massive," he confessed, his voice echoing inside the widespread vacancy. "The darkness looks like an all-ingesting beast, and I... I am only a man with phrases on a page." Her form shimmering with an airy light, Seraph met his gaze with a warmth that cut through his depression. "The burden isn't yours on me, Enoch," she said, her voice calming. "You are a conduit, a bridge for the forgotten language to flow back into the arena. Imagine not an unmarried flame but one thousand embers waiting to be ignited." Her words, even though enigmatic, offered a flicker of desire. He was not supposed to be a solitary beacon but a catalyst. The forgotten language was not just words but a philosophy, a manner of existence that fostered admiration for the divine and the delicate stability of the world. Simply perhaps, he could rekindle that forgotten connection inside fellows' hearts. Leaving the heavenly realm at the back, Enoch felt a tremor of unease settle in his belly. He was not a shepherd leading a flock. He became a lone spark venturing into a good-sized, desolate landscape. Yet, amidst the doubt, a sliver of solutions started to form. He would not be a charismatic leader but a teacher, a weaver of forgotten knowledge. He ventured into the sector, the inscription warm towards his palm, a regular reminder of his daunting undertaking. The first metropolis he visited changed into a microcosm of the depression he was meant to fight. Faces etched with worry; groups fractured through worry – a testimony to the darkness that had taken root. His voice resonated with a newfound urgency as he spoke the forgotten language. He was not just translating words; he was tapping into a wealth of information, a connection to a time when humanity and the divine coexisted in harmony. He saw a flicker of reputation in a few eyes, a craving for something higher. But in others, there was the simplest suspicion, a dismissal of his phrases as the ramblings of a madman. The journey ahead stretched earlier than him, an unsure course fraught with challenges. Self-doubt endured gnawing at him, a steady partner. Yet, with each metropolis he visited, with every flicker of knowledge he ignited, a sliver of wish grew inside him. He became not only a guy but also a bridge walker, the harbinger of a future bathed in the light of a restored covenant. The challenge became daunting, the street in advance perilous, but Enoch, armed with the forgotten language and a developing resolve, might stroll it one step, one flickering ember at a time. He knew the route would not be linear. There could be setbacks, cities that clung to their depression, and groups that were proof against trade. There might be moments when the burden of his challenge would threaten to crush him. But as he traversed the sizable expanse, a new form of courage bloomed within him – the braveness no longer of a warrior but of a quiet revolutionary. He started to look at the forgotten language now as a collection of words and a seed. A seed that could blossom into a collective awakening while planted in fertile ground. He focused on sharing testimonies and rituals, weaving a story of an ancient technology wherein ...Where humanity lived in concord with the divine. He saw a younger boy's eyes widen in awe as he recounted the legend of the heavenly bridge, its shimmering walkway a symbol of the once-shared connection. He saw a seasoned farmer nod in information as he talked about forgotten rituals that commemorated the land. These small victories, those flickering embers of ability, became his fuel, his testimony to the power of the forgotten language. The project remained daunting, the darkness a regular presence lurking at the rims of his journey. Fear and doubt persevered to be his unwelcome companions. But as he walked, he started to apprehend the true nature of his role. He was not supposed to be a novel pressure, a blazing sun that might banish the darkness in one wonderful sweep. He was the moon, a silent yet persistent presence, reflecting the forgotten light onto the sector, one shimmering silver at a time. This realisation brought a degree of peace. He ought to no longer control the results, the tempo of change, or the hearts of folks who listened. But he should manipulate his moves and willpower to share the forgotten language. He will be the steady reminder, the bridge walker, presenting a direction back to the light, even though they chose not to take it now. His journey took him to a bustling town shrouded in smog; its once-vibrant buildings were choked by the fumes of unchecked greed. Here, the forgotten language was not just words but a call to action. Enoch said forgotten rituals commemorated the natural world when era and nature existed in a delicate stability. His phrases were ignored, met with jeers and accusations from a society addicted to development at any price. Disappointment gnawed at him; the burden of his failure was heavy on his shoulders. Yet, as he came to go away, a lone figure approached him. It became a young pupil, his eyes full of desperate hope. "Is there sincerely any other manner?" he asked, his voice slightly a whisper. Enoch saw a reflection of himself in the younger guy's eyes – a yearning for something higher. He found a hand on the pupil's shoulder, his voice filled with quiet conviction. "There is usually another way," he said. "The forgotten language offers now not just phrases, but a choice." Once full of melancholy, the scholar's eyes now held a spark of defiance. It was a small victory, an unmarried ember amidst the darkness, but it was a victory though. Enoch knew that, despite overwhelming odds, the forgotten language held the energy to ignite exchange, one receptive heart at a time. His journey endured, a solitary figure walking toward an unsure horizon. The weight of his project might in no way virtually leave him. Still, now he carried it with a quiet strength, fueled with the aid of the knowledge that even the smallest spark, fanned by using the forgotten language, may want to someday light the arena on fire – a fireplace of knowledge, of concord, of a restored covenant among humanity and the divine.

Enoch's adventure led him through widespread landscapes of wild splendour, where the grandeur of nature mirrored the complexities of his soul. As he ventured deeper into the heart of the unknown, he discovered himself grappling with existential questions that had eluded him. The silence of the desert spoke volumes to his innermost being, urging him to confront his fears and doubts with unflinching honesty. In the stillness of the night, Enoch gazed up at the star-strewn sky, feeling a profound sense of awe at the countless expanse of the universe. He contemplated the mysteries of life and loss of life, of love and the loss of it, looking for solace in the embodiment of the cosmic forces that secure all living beings collectively in a harmonised web of togetherness. With every step he took, Enoch delved deeper into the recesses of his psyche, confronting his internal demons and insecurities with braveness and charm. He discovered that actual growth came no longer from the absence of demanding situations but from the willingness to confront them head-on, embodying the darkness inside as a pathway to the extraordinary. As he journeyed onward, Enoch met fellow tourists whose memories resonated with his very own, every carrying their burdens and joys, a reflection reflecting an extraordinary side of the human experience. Through shared moments of laughter and tears, triumphs and setbacks, Enoch found kinship inside the commonplace threads that secure all of them together in the grand mosaic of life. And so, with a heart full of gratitude and a spirit renewed with the aid of the pains of the street, Enoch persisted in his pilgrimage with a newfound feeling of motive and clarity. He knew that his journey changed far from over and that the road ahead could be fraught with challenges and uncertainties. Still, he confronted it all with a quiet solution born of the understanding that he was no longer alone but became a part of something more than himself.

CHAPTER 18: A GIFT OF CONNECTION

The inscription on Enoch's hand pulsed with an airy light, a legacy stretching back into the mists of time. It was not only a language; it became a birthright, an important weapon in the arsenal of men selected to bridge the distance between humanity and the divine. Enoch had glimpsed fragments – whispers of names carried in the wind, a shared mark on their fingers, a faint echo of forgotten knowledge handed down through generations. Now, as he deciphered the inscription, their memories spread out before him in a breathtaking landscape. There became Adam, the first man entrusted with the heavenly language in its purest shape. He walked with the divine, the language a consistent communication between man and creator. But the concord fractured, a discord whispered inside the Garden of Eden, and the language became a burden, a reminder of a misplaced paradise. Seth, Adam's selected son, inherited the mantle. He was not a warrior or a king but a shepherd of understanding.

He meticulously documented the language, fearing its fading melodies, etching them onto stone drugs and leather-based scrolls. Seth has become the archivist, ensuring the forgotten tongue would not vanish into oblivion. Enoch's gaze lingered on the call of Enosh, a man who walked a distinct route. He was not a scholar or a historian. He changed into a singer and a poet. He used the language to craft hymns of longing, every verse a bridge among the despairing hearts of men and the heavens that appeared to have grown distant. His songs resonated across generations, a testament to the language's power to evoke a longing for the divine. Kenan, the following within the lineage, became a builder. He translated the heavenly principles into tangible structures. He designed temples aligned with the constellations, and every stone meticulously represented the forgotten language. His creations became beacons, physical reminders of the connection humanity once shared with the divine realm. The memories opened, every generation adding a brand-new side to the legacy. Mahalalel, the astronomer, charted the heavens, using the language to decipher the heavenly moves. Jared, the diplomat, used the forgotten tongue to construct bridges among warring tribes, reminding them of the shared humanity etched inside the very material of the language. But the lineage was not without its dark chapters. Methuselah, a man careworn with super toughness, saw the world become chaotic. He has become a cautionary tale, a reminder that the heavenly language was not a magic bullet but a device that needed consistent vigilance and right motion. As Enoch delved deeper, he noticed the connections. Each guy, chosen for their precise capabilities, had stored the legacy alive. The student, the singer, the builder, the astronomer, the diplomat – their diverse tactics have been sides of the entire, a testament to the language's multifaceted nature. And now, it is his turn. Enoch, the bridge walker, was tasked with weaving the forgotten language lower back into the very cloth of human lifestyles. He was not simply confused through the weight of a challenge; he became empowered by the legacy of generations. He carried inside him the archivist's information, the singer's craving, the builder's vision, the astronomer's knowledge, and the diplomat's empathy. He was not by me. He became a part of a lineage, a sequence of men stretching lower back to the sunrise of humanity, all bound with the aid of the heavenly language, all striving to fix the fractured connection between humanity and the divine. The inscription on his hand pulsed with a renewed lightness, no longer a burden but a badge of honour, a testament to his vicinity in a legacy far grander than any single man. With newfound resolve, Enoch stepped out into the sector, ready to weave his verse into the renowned and heralded legacy of the bridge walkers. He would not just be a student or a translator; he might be a weaver, stitching together the fragmented threads of information, reminding humanity of the forgotten music that resonated inside their souls. His journey would not be smooth, but as he looked again at the constellation of names etched in the inscription, he knew he was not taking walks alone. He carried the collective knowledge of generations, a chorus of voices echoing through time, urging him ahead with his challenge to re-ignite the lightness of the heavenly language. The whispers became a steady hum in Enoch's thoughts. Not just the echoes of his predecessors but also the collective voice of humanity craving for a forgotten connection. He travelled not just geographically but in a spiritual transcendence of time. He uncovered forgotten texts penned by his predecessors in historical libraries, each a chunk of the puzzle. He discovered heavenly rituals practised with the aid of Kenan and deciphered astronomical charts left behind with the aid of Mahalalel. He hummed along to dwindled melodies from Enosh's forgotten songs. One day, in a crumbling temple committed to the forgotten language, Enoch stumbled upon a hidden chamber. Inside, a shimmering pool meditated on the starry night sky above.

As he peered into its depths, he felt a presence – now not a divine being, but a collective attention, a wellspring of recollections from people who had walked in that direction earlier than him. Images flooded his mind – Adam walking with heavenly beings in a verdant paradise, Seth meticulously carving symbols on stone, Enosh's voice soaring in a forgotten melody. He no longer felt just their ability, but their emotions – Adam's grief on the misplaced connection, Seth's unwavering dedication, and Enosh's craving for a return to concord. Appearing from the pool, Enoch was now not just a scholar. He changed into a vessel, brimming with the collective knowledge of generations. He understood now. The language was not just words or standards; it changed into an embodiment of the relationship between humanity and the divine, a residing testament to a forgotten connection. He persevered on his journey, but his technique shifted. He did not simply hold forth forgotten words; he shared testimonies, feelings, and the collective memories gleaned from the pool. He sang Enosh's forgotten melodies, their melancholic beauty reawakening a dormant yearning in the hearts of his listeners. He guided farmers in performing rituals passed down with the aid of Kenan, their admiration for the land deepening as they reconnected with the heavenly order. As word of Enoch's deeds spread, a glimmer of wish flickered throughout the land. Communities began to rediscover their forgotten connection to the divine. Farmers who have been ravaged by droughts enacted sustainable practices based totally on historical texts. But the darkness was not without a myriad of problems. Powerful people who thrived on discord and greed noticed their power threatened using the resurgence of the forgotten language. They tried to discredit Enoch, branding him a madman or a heretic. They burned libraries, persecuted his fans, and looked to extinguish the rekindled light. Enoch confronted these challenges with an unwavering remedy. He knew the darkness would combat his lower back. Still, he also knew the forgotten language had awoken something some distance deeper within the hearts of human beings. Just as his predecessors had faced their demanding situations, he would face his. One night, as Enoch sat through a campfire with a group of dependable followers, a young lady approached him. Her eyes, filled with a deep ability, held echoes of the understanding he had obtained from the pool. "You are not by me," she said, her voice sporting the burden of generations. "We are all a part of this, a refrain rising to reclaim the forgotten music." Enoch looked around at the faces illuminated using the flickering fireplace — farmers, artisans, youngsters with a craving in their eyes. He realised the lineage was a chain of people across generations and a growing movement, a collective awakening. He became not simply the bridge walker but the conductor, orchestrating a symphony of forgotten understanding and a craving for a renewed connection. The path beforehand becomes long. Destiny was unsure. But as he looked at the enormous expanse of stars shimmering above, Enoch felt a quiet self-belief. He was part of something larger than himself, a refrain echoing through time. The forgotten language, once a solitary inscription on his hand, now resonated inside the hearts of his fans, a testimony to the iconic power of collective memory and the unwavering human spirit. The bridge he was now committed to building was not simply one man's adventure; it became a bridge built upon generations of knowledge that could someday lead humanity back to the light. Enoch meets a girl who has been related to him all her life and realises she is the only one for him. The caravan bustled with weary tourists seeking respite from the relentless desolate solar tract. Ever the observer, Enoch perched on a weathered crate, watching a younger lady barter with a grizzled merchant. Her fiery purple hair, starkly contrasting to the solar-bleached panorama, bobbed with animation as she argued for a truthful rate on a period of starlit fabric. Something inside her resonated with him, a connection that transcended the din of the market. He caught her eye, and a flicker of reputation, a diffused warm temperature, passed between them. Intrigued, he approached, his voice gentle as he inquired about the material. "It's said to be woven with the threads of forgotten constellations," she answered in her voice, a melody that calmed the desert wind. "They say it can furnish wishes beneath the proper moon." Her eyes, the colouration of twilight shadows, held a depth that startled him. He started the forgotten language, surprised by her immediate knowledge. She said tales handed down to different generations in her family, stories of the bridge walkers and the heavenly tongue. As they talked, the wilderness solar dipped below the horizon, painting the sky in hues of orange and pink. They sat round the campfire, enveloped by the crackling flames and draped by the immense starry sky above them. She talked about her lineage, tracing a constellation sample on her forearm – the identical birthmark adorned Enoch's palm. Then, the whispers of his predecessors coalesced into a resounding truth – she became a descendant of Enosh, the singer. Enoch felt an inexplicable connection bloom inside him. She did not just understand the language; she carried a melody within her soul, a concord that resonated with his personal yearning. He shared tales of his predecessors, of the pool of collective recollections, and she, in turn, shared forgotten songs passed down by ancient voices – historic melodies that evoked a yearning for a bygone era. Days and weeks as they journeyed together. Enoch saw himself counting on her power and unwavering optimism. She, in turn, regarded his knowledge and unwavering determination. They were two halves of an entire bridge, walkers taking walks aspect-by-way, each with a unique legacy piece. One moonlit night, a deeper craving stirred inside Enoch as they camped underneath a luminous full moon. He was not simply attracted to her shared information; he became captivated by her spirit, braveness, and how her laughter chased away the shadows that every now and then clung to him. He no longer wanted only an accomplice in this hard adventure but a partner, a person to share the quiet victories and the crushing disappointments. With a pounding heart, Enoch talented her starlit material. As she draped it over her shoulders, its heavenly threads shimmering inside the moonlight, she seemed imaginative and prescient from the forgotten testimonies. A surprising urge to bridge the distance among them, now not simply in reason but in their hearts, beat him. "There's a forgotten ritual," he began, his voice thick with a combination of nervousness and wish. "A melody intended to bind souls destined to walk the course collectively." Her eyes met his, a query placed inside the air, a query that reflected the one in his personal heart. With a trembling hand, he took hers, his voice resonating with a newfound actuality. "Will you sing this forgotten track with me?" Tears welled up in her eyes as a smile bloomed on her face. At that moment, below the watchful gaze of the heavenly expanse, their voices intertwined, weaving a forgotten melody that resonated with the echoes of generations. It was not only music; it became a promise, a vow to walk the route together, not simply as bridge walkers, but as two souls destined to be one. The journey that lay beforehand changed into exhausting, filled with demanding situations and setbacks. Powerful guys threatened their efforts, clinging to the darkness the forgotten language looked to dispel. Yet, Enoch now does not walk by himself. He had a partner, a bridge walker by his face, her unwavering spirit, and a constant energy supply. They had been no longer just a bridge walker and his follower; they had been melodies woven into one, a testimony to the iconic electricity of love, legacy, and the forgotten language that bound them together. They were a bridge, no longer simply between humanity and the divine, but among hearts, forever entwined in the intimate nature of their shared destiny. Their love story was not a grand, sweeping affair; it changed into a quiet melody woven into the material of their task. They found solace in shared understanding, whispered secrets under starry nights, and deep information that transcended words. It becomes a love built on respect, shared motive, and the unwavering notion that they could re-light the forgotten light together. As they walked hand-in-hand, the inscription on Enoch's hand felt much less like a burden and more like a promise to honour the legacy of the bridge walkers, to reawaken ...The forgotten connection and to construct a future bathed inside the mind of a renewed covenant, all with the girl who sang the forgotten song again into his heart. Their adventure lower back was not a straightforward march to victory but a meticulous journey characterised by layers of quiet victories and shared burdens. They left the wilderness with a band of fans, their numbers growing like wildflowers interested in the solar with every village they touched. Yet, amidst the fervour of rekindled religion and the flicker of desire rekindled in human hearts, a specific form of connection blossomed between Enoch and Zehira, the lady with fiery hair and a song woven into her soul. It was not a sudden spark that ignited their hearts. Still, a sluggish ember, fanned by the shared understanding, whispered among them under starlit skies. Enoch, a person of quiet contemplation, was drawn to Zehira's laughter. This melody chased away the shadows of doubt that sometimes clung to him. He marvelled at her braveness in the face of risk, a clear reflection of his personal development and a power that complemented his flawlessness. One night, huddled around a crackling hearth after a skirmish with bandits threatening a village, Enoch confided in Zehira on the burden of the legacy he carried. He mentioned his predecessors, their triumphs and disasters echoing for a while, the loneliness that now and again gnawed at him despite his undertaking. Zehira listened closely, her eyes reflecting the dancing flames as if they held stories on their own. "You aren't alone," she said, her voice soft but firm, a testimony to the unwavering spirit that reflected his very own. "We are all bridge walkers, every generation sporting a chunk of the forgotten song." She took his hand, tracing the constellation birthmark with a gentle thumb, the contact sending a tremor through him. "We walk collectively, each word complementing the other, developing a concord which could reach even the maximum jaded heart." Her words resonated with him, a relaxing balm to his anxieties. He realised that while he changed into the bridge walker, she became the tune that stuffed it with life. It was not translating forgotten words; it had transcended into relaying a revered message that resonated with the very soul. With newfound self-assurance, Enoch started incorporating Zehira's knowledge into his teachings. They sang forgotten lullabies to soothe the troubled, their voices intertwining in a melody that resonated with a forgotten generation of peace. This harmony calmed children and the anxieties of an international teetering on the threshold. As they traversed fertile plains and climbed snow-capped mountains, their bond deepened. They discovered each different rhythm, and unstated gestures changed lengthy motives. Zehira deciphered historical texts with an uncanny intuition, her voice a natural conduit for the forgotten tongue. Enoch, in turn, marvelled at her ability to translate the heavenly language into realistic rituals that resonated with the not-unusual people. He witnessed how her colourful spirit ignited a spark inside the eyes of even the most jaded villager. This spark grew into a yearning for a higher future. One moonlit night, perched atop a windswept cliff overlooking a slumbering village bathed within the airy glow of the heavenly expanse, Enoch felt an amazing urge to bridge the space between them, not just as bridge walkers but as souls intertwined. He confessed his feelings, his voice raw with emotion, laying bare the vulnerability hidden under his scholarly demeanour. Zehira did not hesitate. She saw the forgotten ritual she had created — a rite that bound souls destined to walk in a direction together, their blended harmonies amplifying the power of their project. Under the watchful gaze of a million stars, they carried out the forgotten ritual. A warm temperature bloomed inside them as their voices merged in the historic melody, confirming the bond that transcended mere phrases. It was not a grand declaration of love underneath a synthetic spotlight but a quiet vow, a promise etched within the language of shared motive and unwavering devotion. Their love tale was not a distraction from their mission; it became a supply of strength, a flickering candle within the darkness that fueled their remedy. They confronted setbacks – villages clinging to superstition, effective figures threatened by the resurgence of the forgotten language and the dismantling of the manipulation they held over the hearts and minds of men. But through all of it, they had each other. At some stage in a hectic negotiation, a stolen appearance, a comforting touch after a long day full of the arduous assignment of rebuilding trust and knowledge – those insignificant gestures became their anchors in a global teetering on the brink. Their journey persisted, a testimony to the long-lasting energy of love and legacy. They were not only a bridge walker and his follower; they were a duet, two voices woven into one, a melody that resonated with the forgotten music snoozing within the hearts of humanity. They were a bridge, now not simply between humanity and the divine, but among souls destined to stroll together. Their love story is a quiet verse within the grand saga of the bridge walkers. As they ventured onwards, the inscription on Enoch's hand did not feel like a ...Burden. Still, a beacon, guiding them toward a future bathed in a renewed covenant's mind. The weight of his assignment now felt lighter, shared with Zehira. He was not just carrying the torch of forgotten knowledge; he walked with a partner, their blended flames burning brighter than either may want to have on my own. They had been a testament to the forgotten language's actual reason – not simply the healing of verbal exchange between humanity and the divine, but the fostering of connection, knowledge, and love – a love tale written no longer just in stolen glances and whispered promises, but within the shared cause of rebuilding a global teetering on the threshold. Enoch stood at the brink of the forest, the light of the setting solar filtering through the bushes in an enchanting dance of colours. As shadows lengthened and the arena around him started to be cloaked within the velvet embody of twilight, Enoch felt a profound experience of peace settle within him. The whispers of the wind rustled through the leaves, carrying with them the ancient songs of the earth. It became as if the very land spoke to him, revealing secrets and knowledge hidden for aeons. Enoch closed his eyes and allowed himself to be over-excited by the symphony of nature, feeling a deep connection to the heartbeat of life that coursed through the land. Enoch felt he was on the cusp of a profound revelation in that moment of stillness. The barriers between the bodily international and the world of the divine seemed to blur, and he sensed a presence, ancient and smart, watching over him with benevolence. The forest spirits had collected around him, offering their courage and safety in this sacred space. The sky above darkened because the stars began to appear, twinkling like beacons of light inside the good-sized expanse of the cosmos. Enoch was overcome with humility in the face of such limitless splendour, understanding how small and insignificant he changed into in the universe's grand scheme. And yet, in that recognition, he also understood the profound connection between all beings, each a fibre woven together to create a stunning masterpiece. As he opened his eyes another time, an experience of peace settled inside him. The weight of the divine presence surrounding him felt like a comforting incite, guiding him toward self-discovery and enlightenment. With a heart full of gratitude and reverence, Enoch embraced his connection to the universe, equipped to embark on a journey of exploration and ability that might lead him to the very heart of life itself.

CHAPTER 19: WALKING THE CHOSEN PATH

Dust swirled around Enoch's boots as he approached the familiar silhouette of his village nestled towards the rolling hills. It had been years given that he had set out, a pupil confused through an inscription and a prophecy. Now, he is back a bridge walker, his heart heavy with memories of a world craving the forgotten language. The village, once colourful, bore the scars of an overlooked settlement. Houses stood empty, fields lay fallow, and a thick pall of despair hung inside the air. Despair grew to become disbelief as Enoch entered the market. People, their faces etched with hardship, stared at him, their preliminary surprise melting into a flicker of reputation. The birthmark on his hand, once a source of fearful interest, now held newfound importance. A vintage female, her face creased with sorrow, approached him, her voice trembling. "Are you… the harbinger?" she asked. Enoch nodded, his throat tight with emotion. He spoke now not of grand or divine pronouncements but of the forgotten stories he had gathered, the rituals that honoured the land, the songs that rekindled a reference to the heavens. He mentioned Zehira, his voice softening as he described her understanding and unwavering spirit. Words unfold like wildfire. People starved for desire amassed around him, their eyes brimming with a yearning for something better. He did not preach; he shared. He shared forgotten songs, their melodies washing over the marketplace, a bomb on their weary souls. He taught them rituals, their moves, a reconnection with the land, and the unseen forces that ruled their lives. Days changed into weeks as he tirelessly shared the forgotten language. A young farmer, stimulated by a heavenly ritual, experimented with ancient crop practices, a ripple impact spreading throughout the community. A talented weaver, guided by ancient blueprints, crafted objects that resonated with a forgotten concord, their splendour a beacon of wish in a desolate landscape. One evening, a delegation approached him as Enoch sat using his aspect with the aid of a crackling hearth with Zehira. It became the village elders, their faces not etched with melancholy but with a newfound admiration. The chief, thick with emotion, spoke: "Enoch, you have lower back not simply with knowledge but with a lightness that has chased away the darkness that clouded our hearts." In that second, the weight of years lifted from Enoch's shoulders. He was not only a bridge walker anymore; he became their bridge and returned to a life of harmony and purpose. The forgotten language, once an inscription on his hand, now resonated inside the voices of his humans, a testimony to the collective attempt it took to rebuild a shattered global. The following day, the very air crackled with a renewed energy. The village gathered within the market, and their faces turned toward Enoch and Zehira's status together. He spoke, not simply as a student back but as a son who had rediscovered his roots. He said the importance of remembering, living in harmony with the sector, and the forgotten connection that ensures all of them are together. He did not call for a revolution but a renaissance – a rebirth of their culture, values, and connection to the divine. Once a burden, the inscription on his hand pulsed with a newfound light, a mirrored image of the wish that now flickered in each eye. As the final words left his lips, a thunderous cheer erupted, a legitimate voice that echoed through the valley, a testimony to their newfound desire. Children danced and blended their laughter into a melody that chased away the shadows of the past. Elders, their faces etched with the information of a difficult existence, nodded in agreement, their eyes glistening with tears. Enoch was not simply hailed as a hero that day; he changed into embraced as a son, a brother, and a shepherd who had guided his flock lower back to a lifestyle bathed within the light of the forgotten language. His journey may also have started as a solitary burden but ended as a shared achievement. It testified to the long-lasting energy of knowledge, affection like the bond he shared with Zehira, and the unwavering spirit of a people craving to be free. It became a victory for Enoch and for generations of bridge walkers who had carried the torch of the forgotten language. This victory promised a future packed with the echoes of a renewed covenant between humanity and the divine. News of the village's renaissance unfolds like wildfire. People from neighbouring settlements, their villages suffering beneath a load of melancholy, started to reach. Enoch and Zehira, no longer burdened by the weight of secrecy, shared their understanding freely. Slowly, a wave of trade began to ripple outwards, carrying on the forgotten language, a testament to the transformative power of an unmarried pupil, a bridge walker, and the female who sang with lower back into his heart. The ripples of change emanating from Enoch and Zehira's village travelled everywhere. Once isolated communities, their spirits dimmed by the darkness that had shrouded the forgotten language began to re-light the embers of hope. Delegations arrived, searching for not just information but steering. Enoch, in no way one to turn away from his obligation, effortlessly shared the forgotten understanding. However, the resurgence of the heavenly tongue was no longer going unnoticed. Powerful figures who thrived on discord and management saw their empires threatened. Whispers of rebellion opposing their iron grip began to thrust upward, fueled by the newfound harmony that the forgotten language fostered. Plots have been hatched in the shadows, machinations designed to extinguish the flickering light. One day, a cloaked discern arrived in Enoch's village. The air crackled with a feeling of foreboding as the determined approached him. It became a messenger from the High Chancellor, the most effective man in the land, whose grip on facts and resources had choked the lifestyles out of countless communities. The message was simple: quit your teachings or face the effects. His hand was instinctively going to the inscription thrummed with renewed strength. Enoch knew he could not back down. He answered with quiet solve, refusing to be cowed by threats. News of the High Chancellor's ultimatum spread like wildfire. A wave of anger, fueled by the aid of years of oppression, surged through the villages that had determined solace within the forgotten language. Enoch, realising this was not simply his fight anymore, known as for a meeting. People from all walks of lifestyles, their faces etched with a newfound dedication, arrived. Farmers came with pitchforks, artisans with their gear, and youngsters with their voices, equipped to sing the melodies of a forgotten generation. The atmosphere crackled with a tension that was both hopeful and dangerous. Enoch addressed the group, his voice unwavering. He talked about the legacy of the bridge walkers, of generations who had stored the flame alive. He said Zehira, his voice softening as he described her unwavering spirit, an image of the unity they were fighting for. "Today," he declared, his voice growing above the murmur, "we stand together, no longer as isolated villages but as a network held by the forgotten language. They may also try to silence us, but our voices will not be drowned out. We will sing the forgotten music so loudly that its echoes will reach the heavens themselves!" A collective roar rang through the valley, a testament to their solidarity. They knew the fight would not be easy, but they would not back down. They had tasted freedom, and the forgotten language had appeared as the armour that shielded their hearts. The following days have been a blur of pastime. They devised techniques, practised peaceful resistance, and readied themselves for anything that would come. Enoch, Zehira, by using his face, served as their chief, his scholarly knowledge interwoven with the realistic abilities he had gotten on his journey. Finally, the day of reckoning arrived. The High Chancellor's military, an impressive force shrouded in darkness, descended upon the village. Fear threatened to engulf the crowd, but his gaze locked on Zehira's unwavering eyes. Enoch saw a flicker of defiance inside the people's faces. The squaddies advanced, their swords glinting underneath the harsh sunlight. But as opposed to worry, a ripple of defiance unfolds through the assembled mass. They did not fight with weapons but with words. They sang the forgotten songs, their melodies creating an enchanting sequence of harmony and rhythm that reverberated throughout the valley. They recited ancient rituals, their voices a chorus of defiance against the encroaching darkness. The infantry soldiers faltered and harassed using the sudden resistance. The forgotten language, designed for verbal exchange and connection, stirred something inside them. Memories of forgotten testimonies, of a time whilst humanity lived in concord with the land and the divine, surfaced in their minds. One by using one, soldiers decreased their weapons. Some even joined the chorus, their voices melding with the villagers in a melody that saw hope and cohesion. The tide had turned. The High Chancellor's plans had crumbled within the face of the forgotten language's unifying strength. News of the nonviolent rebel spread like wildfire, igniting a spark of defiance across the land. Villages rose towards their oppressors, wielding not guns but the forgotten language. The darkness that had shrouded the land for goodbye started to recede, defeated by a glimmer of hope. Enoch and Zehira, their journey that began as a solitary task and is now a catalyst for tremendous change, watched the sunrise rise over a hopeful destiny. They knew the street beforehand would not be clean. Still, the forgotten language, a bridge between humanity and the divine and among hearts, became an effective device of their hands. They are no longer bridge walkers; they have been architects, rebuilding an international where humanity and the divine ought to coexist in harmony another time, their voices intertwined in a forgotten tune that now echoes as an effective ...Symphony throughout the land. The inscription on Enoch's hand, once a burden, now glowed with celestial light, a beacon not just for him but for generations to come back. It was a steady reminder of his legacy, not of a single bridge walker but of a collective spirit that refused to be silenced. Years passed, and the forgotten language bloomed anew. Children found ancient songs in colleges, farmers used heavenly rituals to guide their cultivation, and artisans crafted items imbued with the forgotten harmony. The land, once ravaged with the aid of forgotten spirits, flourished under the care of human beings reconnected to its rhythms. Enoch and Zehira, their love tale woven into the material of this renaissance, grew old together. They continued to journey, now not as weary pupils but revered elders, sharing their knowledge and reminding humans of the electricity of team spirit and the forgotten language. The inscription on Enoch's hand, a faint echo on his wrinkled skin, served as a regular reminder of their journey — a testimony to the enduring electricity of a single voice, a love that confounded odds, and a legacy that had bridged the gap among a forgotten beyond and a hopeful future. One evening, as they sat by a crackling fire, watching a new generation sing the forgotten songs underneath a starlit sky, Zehira leaned her head on Enoch's shoulder. "We did it," she whispered, her voice laced with contentment. Enoch smiled, his eyes crinkling in one corner. "We did," he agreed, squeezing her hand. "Together." In that quiet second, surrounded by the melody of a rekindled global, they knew their adventure, a testimony to love, legacy, and the forgotten language, had come full circle. The bridge that they had built was not just one among stone and mortar. Still, it was a bridge of hearts that had led humanity to return to the light, a light that would hold to polish for generations to come back. Enoch starts evolving to teach the lost phrase to young humans in his town to ensure it is not forgotten. The midday solar beat down on the bustling market, casting long shadows that danced with kids' laughter.

Enoch, his weathered face etched with a grin, stood below the colour of a sprawling fig tree. Around him, a bunch of youngsters, their eyes huge with curiosity, sat cross-legged on worn rugs unfolding on the dusty floor. This was not a traditional lesson. Enoch was not teaching them the names of veggies or the intricacies of mathematics. He looked like he was about to impart a treasure far more precious — the misplaced phrase. He started by drawing a symbol inside the dust with his gnarled finger — a circle bisected by a line. This easy but profound image stood for the forgotten word's essence. "This, my kids," he introduced, his voice warm and inviting, "is the symbol for 'Keshura'." A murmur rippled through the institution. Keshura. The phrase felt foreign on their tongues, yet something deep within them resonated. Enoch explained that Keshura was not only a word; it became an idea — a harmonious connection among humanity, the land, and the heavenly realm. It referred to a balance, a way of living that revered the earth and acknowledged the divine. He went on to tell stories, handed down through generations of bridge walkers, of a time when Keshura guided every issue of existence. Farmers planted their vegetation using ancient techniques, their movements mirroring the dance of the celebs. Artisans crafted objects imbued with the spirit of Keshura, their creations fostering a sense of peace and concord with the herbal international. Even the simplest duties, like weaving baskets or tending to a fire, have been revered for this forgotten concept. Enoch's voice resonated with a quiet ardour as he noted the gradual decline of Keshura and how its means became misplaced in the din of day-by-day lifestyles. The children listened carefully, their faces a combination of fascination and unhappiness. But Enoch was not simply weaving a story of a lost past. He changed into constructing a bridge to the future. He taught them easy chants within the forgotten language, melodies that carried the essence of Keshura. They practised incorporating the concept into their day-by-day lives – from planting seeds in alignment with the levels of the moon to crafting items with a mindful admiration for the materials they used. Enoch saw a metamorphosis that stretched past the market as days became weeks. Once content with aimless games, the kids approached their chores with a newfound motive. Inspired by Enoch's teachings, a younger shepherd began leaving offerings of gratitude to the heavenly bodies as he watched over his flock. A young weaver, fascinated by the forgotten language's connection to the herbal international, experimented with dyes extracted from local flowers, their vibrant hues making a song a silent harmony with the panorama. One night, as Enoch sat with the aid of the fireplace with Zehira, a younger lady named Elara approached him, her eyes gleaming. "Enoch," she said, her voice full of a newfound self-belief, "nowadays, once I helped my mom plant the seeds, I felt Keshura. I felt the earth reply and knew it might nourish our vegetation." Enoch's heart swelled with delight. This was not about teaching a word; it became the reawakening of a dormant part of their souls. Zehira squeezed his hand, her smile mirroring his personal. "They're gaining knowledge of," she whispered, "now not just the word, but the feeling in the back of it." It becomes a sense of connection, belonging, and an experience of being a part of something larger than themselves. Enoch knew his adventure was not over as the hearth crackled and the celebs appeared within the tremendous expanse above. He might preserve to teach, to share the forgotten language and the invaluable idea of Keshura. He would plant the seeds of knowledge now inside the hearts of these younger minds and within the very fabric of their society. He envisioned a destiny where children discovered the forgotten songs in colleges, farmers used heavenly rituals to manual their cultivation practices, and artisans crafted objects imbued with the forgotten harmony. Enoch knew the path forward would not be clean. There might be those who clung to the old methods, who feared the strength of a reawakened Keshura. But with each infant who grasped the essence of the forgotten phrase, with every new era that found out to stay in harmony with the land and the divine, Enoch felt a developing experience of desire. He changed into no longer just a bridge walker; he became a seed planter, sowing the seeds of a destiny bathed in the light of a renewed covenant, a destiny in which the forgotten language, once a solitary inscription on his hand, could resonate as a triumphant symphony across the hearts of generations to come. Enoch walked alongside the dusty path; his steps guided through a sense of purpose that resonated deep inside his soul. The weight of responsibility lay heavy upon his shoulders, yet he carried it with willpower and resolve. As he journeyed on, Enoch considered the divine message bestowed on him. The encounter that had changed the route of his life for all time had taken a region underneath the cover of a tree, where the smooth whispers of the wind had carried the words of his destiny to him. He should still feel the tingling strength that had enveloped him, filling him with awe and reverence. Enoch knew his venture had become a non-public calling and a sacred obligation. The assignments entrusted to him became more than himself, and he felt humbled by the size of the responsibility placed on his shoulders. Yet, deep inside his heart, he also felt an experience of gratitude for being chosen for this sacred motive. The road ahead became fraught with demanding situations and barriers, but Enoch's faith never wavered. He drew strength from the historical understanding, a legacy of understanding and religious belief cultivated over generations. With every step he took, Enoch felt a deep connection to the land around him, the trees that whispered ancient secrets and techniques, and the celebs that shone brightly within the night sky. He knew that he had become a part of a bigger picture, painted with strokes of destiny and cause and that his function became a small but large part of the universe's grand design. As he persevered on his adventure, Enoch embraced the challenges ahead with a sense of peace and readability. He understood that his path had changed into something not constantly smooth. Still, he also knew that every trial and tribulation served a greater cause inside the grand scheme of factors. Enoch's thoughts wandered to the teachings of the ancient sages, who had imparted the secrets of the cosmos and the mysteries of the human spirit. Their phrases echoed in his thoughts, guiding him on his quest with a feeling of wisdom past his years. The sky above him darkened because the sun dipped below the horizon, portraying the sector in colours of red and gold. Enoch felt a sense of awe at the splendour of creation, the vastness of the universe, and the complicated net of life that linked all beings. With a heart full of gratitude and a soul set alight with motive, Enoch persevered on his journey, eager to find out what mysteries lay ahead and what wonders awaited him on the path that stretched out earlier than him.

CHAPTER 20: THE UNFOLDING OF DIVINE VISIONS

A wave of vertigo washed over Enoch as he knelt beside the shimmering pool inside the forgotten temple. The air crackled with a forgotten strength, and the flickering torchlight danced unevenly on the water's surface. He had deciphered the historical rituals, spoken the forgotten phrases, and now, with a pounding heart, awaited the knowledge the pool promised. Then, it began. The water swirled, coalescing into a swirling vortex. Images flickered, fleeting at the beginning, then solidifying into a scene. An extensive, bustling town stretched before him, its towers reaching for the heavens like steel palms clawing at the sky. People of all colours and creeds moved with a frenetic strength, a ceaseless hum of pastime that vibrated through the air. Yet, a discordant note echoed underneath the surface. The air shimmered with a haze that stung Enoch's eyes, and the land itself regarded weary, its once vibrant hues muted by using a cloak of pollutants. A sense of alienation hung heavy inside the air, a hollowness gnawed at Enoch's soul. People bustled beyond each other, their faces etched with a loneliness that transcended the throngs. The vision dissolved all at once because it seemed, leaving at the back of a profound experience of unease. Enoch appeared from the pool, his frame trembling, the weight of the imaginative and prescient clinging to him like a shroud. Zehira rushed to him, her eyes filled with a challenge that reflected his turmoil. "What did you spot?" she asked, her voice barely a whisper. He defined the imaginative and prescient, his phrases tinged with a newfound dread. "A town of wonders," he rasped, "but without connection. People dwelling in abundance, yet desperately lonely." He checked out Zehira, his heart heavy with a burden he now shared. "Is this our future?" Zehira, ever the optimist, placed a hand on his arm, her contact a grounding force amidst the swirling typhoon of feelings. "Destiny is not always set in stone, Enoch," she said lightly. "These visions are warnings, not prophecies. They are a glimpse of what can be if we fail to learn from the beyond." Enoch took a deep breath, his remedy hardening right into a burning ember within him. "Then we have to educate them," he declared, his voice ringing with newfound purpose. "We must teach them the forgotten language, the idea of Keshura – the connection between humanity, the land, and the divine. Only then can we keep away from this desolate future." He knew this became the primary vision, a harrowing glimpse of their future capability paths. He steeled himself, geared up to stand something knowledge the pool had to offer, understanding that with every imaginative and prescient, he could be armed with a fraction of the destiny, a chunk of the puzzle he now bore the duty to resolve. The weight of this newfound understanding settled upon him, but it became a burden he became inclined to bear. He became a bridge walker, and this was the bridge he was destined to move. The memory of the first imaginative and prescient, sprawling, lonely metropolis lingered in Enoch's mind like a terrible dream. He sat by using the pool all over again, the inscription on his hand pulsing with an expectant warm temperature. With Zehira through his aspect, his hand clasped in hers, he ventured back into the swirling depths of the pool. This time, the vision unfolded in stark comparison to the primary. A large-sized wilderness stretched before him, an infinite expanse of sand dunes bleached white underneath the relentless sun. The sky, a canvas of bleached turquoise, presented no respite, and a bone-chilling wind whipped sand towards his face. In the gap, he noticed the skeletal remains of what were once extremely vibrant cities, crumbling monuments to a forgotten civilization. A lone discern trudged through the desolate panorama, his return bent with the burden of depression. His clothes have been tattered; his face has weathered past his years. As the figure approached, Enoch recognized the desperation etched in his eyes – a thirst no longer only for water but for that means, for connection in an international without existence. Suddenly, the imaginative and prescient shifted, specialising in a single plant suffering to continue living in harsh surroundings. Its leaves were brittle, its stem gnarled. Yet, it clung tenaciously to lifestyles, its roots looking desperately for the final vestiges of moisture. An unmarried, shrunk fruit clung precariously to a branch, a testimony to the plant's resilience in the face of overwhelming odds. The imaginative and prescient dissolved as unexpectedly as it appeared, leaving Enoch feeling profound disappointment. The future he had seen became one in every one of environmental devastation, a world ravaged by misfortune and without the harmony he so fervently hoped to restore. "This cannot be it," Zehira whispered, her voice trembling slightly. "We cannot allow this to occur." Enoch nodded, a newfound urgency flickering in his eyes. "The forgotten language," he said, his voice corporation, "it's now not just about connecting humanity to the divine. It reminds them of their obligation to the land and the delicate stability that sustains all existence." He looked at the inscription in his hand, the pulsating warm temperature seeming to heighten. "The bridge we are building," he persisted, "isn't just among humanity and the heavens, but among ourselves and the earth. We need to learn to stay in harmony with nature, no longer exploit it."

The second was vivid and visionary, and it served as a stark reminder of the results of ignoring the forgotten language's central standards. It became a destiny without Keshura, a global one in which humanity had severed its connection with the land, leading to a desolate and unforgiving international situation. The weight of responsibility pressed closely upon them, but it also fueled their resolve. They could no longer allow this future to come to skip. With every imagination and visionary, their ventures have become clearer, the load heavier, yet the purpose more compelling. The forgotten language was not just a key to a forgotten beyond; it became important to securing their future. The swirling vortex in the pool all over again flickered to life, beckoning Enoch and Zehira back into its depths. This time, the imaginative and prescient that opened was now not one in all sizable landscapes but of a confined space – a brightly lit room packed with rows upon rows of equal pods. Within every pod, a human parent lay immobile, their faces faded and expressionless. Wires snaked from the pods, connecting them to a widespread network of buzzing machines that crammed the room with a low, monotonous drone. A figure cloaked in white walked among the pods, their actions particular and indifferent. They spoke in a language without inflexion, their phrases sterile and technical. As Enoch watched, the determined in white inserted a glowing orb into a slot on one of the pods. The orb pulsed with an otherworldly lightness, and the determination in the pod stirred, a flicker of popularity changing the blankness in their eyes. Enoch recoiled, a wave of nausea washing over him. This was not a destiny of devastation; it became a destiny of management. Here, humanity was not wiped out; they have been subdued, their minds plugged into a device that dictated their minds, feelings, and lifestyles. The forgotten language, the idea of Keshura, the connection to the land and the divine, controlled utopia. A sense of claustrophobia gripped Enoch. He longed for the warm temperature of the sun on his pores and skin, the texture of the earth underneath his feet, and the connection to the great unknown above. This destiny felt like a prison, an international one in which individuality had been sacrificed for the sake of order and performance. The vision ended as abruptly as it began, leaving him breathless and disoriented. Zehira, her face etched with a combination of fear and anger, looked at him. "This is the worst, but," she whispered. "A global where humanity turns into a gadget, their minds and spirits as controlled as the pods they inhabit." Enoch nodded, his voice tight with loathing. "They've forgotten more than the language," he rasped. "They've forgotten what it means to be human." The inscription on his hand throbbed with a renewed intensity. More than the others, this imaginative and prescient highlighted the significance of the forgotten language. It was not about knowledge or ritual; it became preserving their essence as people, their ability for impartial notion, and their connection to the sector around them. In the face of this potential destiny, the forgotten language was not just a lost treasure; it became a weapon, a shield against the encroaching tide of control and conformity. Enoch knew the battle for the future had become even more pressing. This was not a forgotten manner of lifestyles; it changed into the very soul of humanity. He looked at Zehira, a fierce determination changing the concern in her eyes. Together, they faced the churning pool, geared up to confront whatever visions awaited them, understanding that with each glimpse of a potential destiny, they had been collecting the expertise and the will to construct a one-of-a-kind one – a destiny bathed within the light of the forgotten language. In this future, humanity thrived no longer in sterile pods but inside the vibrant symphony of Keshura. Enoch and Zehira braced themselves as they approached the shimmering pool. The weight of the earlier visions hung heavy, every stark portrayal of a future long past awry. This time, the swirling vortex pulsated with a one-of-a-kind power, a frantic rhythm that mirrored Enoch's pounding heart. The imaginative and prescient that unfolded before them was one of chaos. Towering towns erupted in flames, their metal skeletons twisting towards a smoke-choked sky. Warring factions clashed inside the streets, their guns spitting fire and fury. The air crackled with evil energy, a palpable anxiety that started pressing down on Enoch's soul. As he looked nearer, he noticed the forgotten language twisted and weaponized. Chants, once used to connect to the divine, were now used to fuel the flames of struggle. Symbols of concord had been emblazoned on the banners of warring factions; their original meaning perverted into justifications for violence. This was not a future where the language changed into forgotten; it was a destiny wherein it became corrupted, in which its very essence fueled the destruction of the arena. Enoch felt a wave of despair wash over him. He had predicted misfortune, devastation, even famine, but this – this was a perversion of everything they had been fighting for. The forgotten language, supposed to be a bridge, had now become a weapon tearing the arena aside. Zehira sensed his despair and positioned a comforting hand on his arm. "This is not the most effective path," she whispered, her voice regular despite the scene unfolding before them. "This is a warning, not a prophecy." Enoch clung to her words, looking for a flicker of hope inside the inferno. He saw pockets of resistance, small groups of people still holding onto the forgotten language's real meaning. They used the chants to heal the wounded and the symbols to foster peace negotiations. They have been a beacon of lightness inside the encroaching darkness, a testimony to the long-lasting energy of Keshura. The vision dissolved, leaving behind a sense of chilling urgency. This was no longer about teaching the forgotten language but ensuring it was not misused. They no longer had to teach phrases simply to the spirit behind them - the importance of harmony and living with the world around them. Enoch stared intently at Zehira with remarkable conviction burning in his eyes. "We should be careful," he said, his voice organisation. "Language can be a powerful device, but it can also be a weapon. We have to reveal to them the right way, the direction of Keshura, or this vision may turn out to be true." With a heavy heart, Enoch knew the adventure would not be smooth. The ability for misuse lurked within the phrases they sought to preserve. He had to stroll a tightrope, ensuring the information became shared while guarding against its corruption. The inscription on his hand pulsed with a renewed warmness, a steady reminder of the duty they shouldered, the delicate stability they needed to hold. The fourth vision was not just a glimpse of destiny; it became a project. They needed to be no longer bridge walkers but guardians, ensuring the bridge they built led to harmony, not destruction. The future of the forgotten language, and with it, the future of humanity, rested on their shoulders. With a deep breath, Enoch and Zehira became far from the pool, geared up to stand this new project, armed with the understanding of the potential pitfalls and the unwavering commitment to the actual course of Keshura. Enoch and Zehira approached the pool again, their faces etched with trepidation and backbone. The visions they had seen to this point painted a chilling portrait of ability futures long past wrong. This time, the swirling vortex inside the pool shimmered with celestial light. This luminescence filled Enoch with a careful wish. As they plunged into the depths of the imaginative and prescient, the scene that opened earlier was not chaos or devastation but of a world bathed in a smooth, golden light. Lush landscapes stretched as far away as the attention could see, vibrant with life. People of all walks of life lived in harmony with nature, their communities nestled amidst rolling hills and verdant forests. Yet, something felt exceptional. The forgotten language was not spoken in bustling marketplaces or chanted in grand rituals. It permeated the very material of their lives. Farmers tilled the land guided through historic heavenly cycles, their moves echoing a forgotten dance with the celebrities. Artisans crafted gadgets infused with an unspoken reverence for the substances they used, their creations resonating with nature's designs. Enoch noticed children playing, their laughter echoing through the valleys. They were not reciting forgotten chants, but their video games have been infused with an innate understanding of the herbal world. They constructed miniature homes in harmony with the glide of the wind, mimicking the strategies used by their ancestors. They sang songs and memorized melodies that echoed the seasons' rhythm. The forgotten language was not a relic of the past; it became a residing, respiratory entity woven into the very cloth of their society. It was not an ability held by a selected few; it became an intuitive knowledge surpassed through generations, an unspoken language of the heart. As the imaginative and prescient started to fade, Enoch felt a surge of wish, a warmth that spread through his chest. This became what he had strived for, the true essence of Keshura – an international in which humanity lived in harmony with the land and the divine, no longer through words by me but through an inherent understanding. Zehira squeezed his hand, her eyes shining with tears of pleasure. "This," she whispered, her voice thick with emotion, " is the destiny we should strive for. A destiny in which the forgotten language lives no longer just in words, but in the hearts of every dwelling being." Enoch nodded, a newfound sense of motivation coursing through him. This was not only about teaching the forgotten language anymore; it was all about fostering a connection, an intuitive ability. He had to expose them to the way of life within them, not just the words. The fifth vision was not only a glad finish; it became a venture, a guiding light for their journey. It confirmed their ability, the last purpose of their challenge. It fueled their remedy to ensure that the forgotten language was not only a key to the past but a bridge to a future bathed in harmony, appreciation, and a deep reference to the sector around them. Leaving the pool behind, Enoch and Zehira stepped again into the prevailing, their hearts brimming with a newfound wish. They would face challenges, resistance, and doubt, but the vision that they had seen served as a beacon, a steady reminder of the destiny they were preventing. They have been no longer bridge walkers; they have been architects, laying the inspiration for a global in which the forgotten language resonated within the very rhythm of their lives - an international one in which humanity and the divine coexisted in a symphony of concord. Enoch and Zehira stood through the pool, their faces drawn with anticipation and apprehension. The 5 visions they had seen had unveiled a kaleidoscope of futures, each a stark portrayal of the effects of forgetting the forgotten language, Keshura. Now, with a deep breath, they plunged into the swirling depths of the sixth imaginative and prescient. This time, the scene that unfolded was not on Earth in any respect. A large, ringed planet hung within the inky blackness of the area, its floor a canvas of swirling blue and white. An embellished with symbols like the forgotten language, a glossy vessel hovered above. Inside, figures clad in shimmering suits moved with practised efficiency. Enoch found them – as human beings, descendants of people who had ventured out into the cosmos generations ago. They had carried the forgotten language with them, its symbols adorning their era, but its essence appeared... hole. They spoke the phrases, but with an indifferent formality, without the reverence and connection, Keshura embodied. They used their knowledge of heavenly terrains for navigation. Still, they were unaware of the well-known divine spark within the stars. They had been masters of the forgotten language but lost their spirit. Enoch watched in growing unease as they approached a planet teeming with lifestyles. Advanced scanners probed the surroundings and their movements without recognising this developing world. They referred to useful resource extraction, their voices devoid of thought for the ability results. A feeling of dread settled upon Enoch. Was this the closing irony? Humanity, having mastered the forgotten language and ventured into the cosmos, had forgotten its middle concepts – the purpose they had sought out the stars inside the first location. Keshura, a bridge to harmony Concord, had appeared as a tool for exploitation. Just as melancholy threatened to devour him, the vision shifted. A lone figure, clad in an easy robe decorated with forgotten language symbols, stood at the vessel's bridge. They seemed out on the alien planet, their eyes filled with a deep reverence. Enoch diagnosed them as a descendant, but one who held onto the authentic essence of Keshura. This lone figure spoke, now not inside the indifferent language of their friends, but in a tongue infused with a deep recognition of existence. They argued for warning, knowledge, and honouring all things' interconnectedness. The imaginative and prescient ended, leaving Enoch and Zehira suspended in a demanding silence. The weight of this imaginative and prescient became different. It was not a destiny of devastation; it changed into a future of ability neglected, of a legacy squandered. They had not just failed on Earth; they had failed the universe. Yet, the lone discern offered a flicker of desire. It became a reminder that even in the depths of development, the essence of Keshura should live on. Enoch looked at Zehira, a silent conversation passing between them. They needed to ensure that the forgotten language was not simply mastered; it had to be understood, loved and lived. The bridge they have been building was not simply between humanity and the land;

it became a bridge between them and the cosmos. Enoch's dreams did not end there, and the sixth one was a stark reminder of the remaining reason for their adventure. It was not about preserving the past; it was a tool in ensuring a destiny where humanity, armed with the ability of Keshura, could mission out into the celebs now not as conquerors but as responsible stewards of the universe. With renewed determination, Enoch and Zehira stepped far away from the pool, prepared to face the demanding situations in advance, understanding that the forgotten language held the key to their beyond and their future among the stars. A heavy silence hung in the air as Enoch and Zehira stood by the shimmering pool. The weight of the six visions they had seen pressed down upon them. Every glimpse of a capable future was shaped by the forgotten language, Keshura. Hope battled with dread. The capability for concord weighed against the perils of misfortune and misuse. This time, as they plunged into the depths of the vision, they were not met with a single sight but an array of scenes from several fragments of time. Images flickered, a kaleidoscope of humanity's adventure. Children sang forgotten songs in bustling cityscapes, melodies bridging the concrete and the cosmos. Farmers in remote fields used historical rituals to guide their planting, their actions echoing a dance with the celebs. Enoch noticed that scholars no longer decoded forgotten language but integrated its knowledge into clinical improvements. Once a manipulation device, technology now hummed with a newfound appreciation for the natural world. The symbols of Keshura were not simply adornments; they had been reminders of the interconnectedness of all things. There had been conflicts of path. Misunderstandings flared, and the ability for misuse remained. But inside this appearance of chaos, Enoch saw a fundamental shift. The forgotten language was not about understanding; it was a verbal exchange, a dialogue between generations, cultures, or even with the unknown. The imaginative and prescient culminated in a panoramic vista. Various organisations of human beings, their faces etched with the testimonies of their ancestors, stood on a hill overlooking a verdant panorama. They spoke one-of-a-kind languages, but a shared understanding resonated in their eyes. They have been bridging walkers, not simply among land and sky, but among hearts and minds. Enoch and Zehira appeared from the pool as the vision dwindled, a profound peace settling upon them. They had seen the capability pitfalls, the capability triumphs. The future was not set in stone; it was a canvas waiting to be painted. "We did it," Zehira whispered, a tear tracing a direction down her cheek. "We confirmed them the way." Enoch nodded, his heart overflowing with quiet pride. Their journey, fraught with risk and uncertainty, had reached its culmination. They had rekindled the flame of the forgotten language, now not simply as a group of phrases but as a philosophy, a manner of existence. The inscription on Enoch's hand nonetheless pulsed with a faint warm temperature, a consistent reminder of the duty they had borne. Now, it felt lighter, a mark of their struggles and the destiny they had helped create. This was not their adventure's stop; it became a fresh start. They would continue to educate, inspire, and remind people of the power of Keshura. But now, they are no longer by themselves. The forgotten language, once a solitary beacon, had become a symphony resonating across generations. This bridge related humanity to its beyond and destiny and to the essence of life. As the sun rose, casting a golden light upon their faces, Enoch and Zehira knew that the tune of Keshura would always echo in the hearts of humanity, a testament to the enduring electricity of a bridge constructed on love, legacy and a language long forgotten. Enoch sat in quiet meditation, his heart open to the whispers of the divine. As he closed his eyes, a flood of images and visions washed over him, each carrying a profound message and a call to movement. He saw a world bathed in a golden light, wherein all beings lived in harmony and harmony. The splendour of this imaginative and prescient delivered tears to his eyes, and he knew that it became a glimpse of the future that would be if humanity selected to stroll the route of love and compassion. But along this shimmering photo, darker visions lurked inside the shadows. Engraved in his thoughts have been scenes of destruction, greed, and strife. Enoch urgently felt the burden of those visions on him, urging him to take a stand and help guide his humans toward a higher destiny. As he delved deeper into the visions, he started apprehending the interconnectedness of all matters. Regardless of how small, each movement rippled throughout the cloth of existence, shaping the arena in visible and unseen approaches. Enoch discovered that he held within him the power to influence these ripples, to persuade them toward a destiny packed with wish and lightness. Guided by a feeling of motive that burned within him like a beacon, Enoch made a solemn vow to grow to be a conduit for the divine messages he had bought. He understood that his course might be fraught with demanding situations and boundaries. Still, he also knew that he changed into now, not on my own, on this sacred journey. The universe itself whispered its guide, a light reassurance that he changed into the right route. With renewed willpower and an experience of awe at the vastness of the cosmos, Enoch appeared from his meditation. The echoes of the divine visions lingered in his mind, filling him with a feeling of urgency and a deep-seated conviction that he was destined to play a pivotal role in the unfolding drama of advent. The weight of this newfound duty settled on his shoulders like a cloak, urging him to step forward and embody his destiny. Enoch felt a surge of strength coursing through his veins, igniting a fire that burned brighter with every passing second. He knew beforehand that the road might be fraught with challenges and boundaries. Still, he also knew he was no longer alone in this sacred journey. The universe whispered its guide, reassuring him that he was on the right course. With a heart full of reason and a spirit alight with divine suggestion, Enoch took his first step closer to enjoying his sacred venture. Each footfall was marked with the weight of his dedication, resonating with the cosmic energies that guided his every flow. And as he walked in the direction of his future, he carried within him the light of 1000 stars, a beacon of desire that shone brightly in the darkness, illuminating the route for all who looked for a better international.

Chapter 21: The Torch Bearer

The whole city gathered and stood still. Enoch, his weathered face laced with newfound wisdom, stood upon a makeshift platform. Amara, her hand clasped firmly in his, stood beside him, a silent pillar of support. He did not overwhelm them with grand pronouncements of the future or apocalyptic warnings. Instead, he began by sharing captivating stories with them. He spoke of the thriving cities he had seen in his visions, where people bustled with an almost frantic energy yet felt a profound loneliness gnawing at their souls. He described the desolate wasteland as a stark reminder of the consequences of neglecting the earth and its delicate balance. He spoke of the sterile pods, a future where humanity became purposeless, devoid of spirit and connection. With each tale, a collective gasp rippled through the crowd. Fear and introspection, raw and real, replaced the first curiosity. The stories were not meant to frighten but to awaken. They were a glimpse into the potential consequences of ignoring the forgotten language, Keshura, the bridge between humanity, the land, and the divine. Then, Enoch shifted his focus. He spoke of the future where the forgotten language thrived, a future bathed in the light of Keshura. He described children singing songs honouring the earth, farmers guided by rituals, and artisans crafting objects imbued with respect for the materials they used. A wave of hope washed over the town square. This was a future they could strive for, where humanity was surviving and thriving in harmony with the world around them. Enoch did not stop with just stories, though. He knew true change required action, a shift in perspective that transcended mere words. He begins with simple practices, weaving the forgotten language into the fabric of their daily lives. He taught them chants to connect with the land, heavenly alignments for planting, and ways to infuse daily tasks with the spirit of Keshura. The marketplace transformed into a vibrant classroom. Farmers, weary of diminishing harvests, learned to work with the earth's rhythms, their movements mirroring the dance of the stars in the sky. Inspired by a renewed reverence for nature, artisans started crafting objects that served a purpose beyond mere utility. Their creations sang with an earthly beauty, a testament to the forgotten language's influence. Children's laughter echoed through the square, and they sang the forgotten songs during their games. These were not just melodies; they were stories passed down through generations, an innate understanding of the world woven into the very fabric of their play. Scepticism, of course, remained. Some clung to old ways, fearing change and the unfamiliar. But as the seasons turned, the results spoke for themselves. Crops flourished, nourished by practices attuned to heavenly cycles. Craftsmanship rose to a new level, imbuing their creations with a beauty that resonated with the soul. And most importantly, a sense of community blossomed, replacing the fractured relationships of the past. People began to see each other not as competitors but as collaborators in a shared dance with nature. One evening, as the setting sun painted the sky in hues of orange and gold, Enoch sat by the fire with Amara. The town square buzzed with a newfound energy, a symphony of laughter and purpose. It was not just the din of a bustling marketplace; it was the harmonious song of a community reconnected with itself and the world around it. "They're learning," Amara said, her voice filled with contentment, not just with their progress but the journey itself. They had faced challenges, fear, and doubt but appeared stronger, and their bond and purpose solidified. Enoch smiled. He had seen the future, all the paths their world could take. Now, he was shaping a future where the bridge he had crossed – the bridge between humanity, the land, and the divine – was not just his journey but a shared path for future generations. The wisdom he gleaned from the pool was not just knowledge but a responsibility. He was a bridge walker, but now he was also a guide, leading his people not towards a set destination but towards a way of living that echoed in the forgotten language, resonating with the very heartbeat of the universe. The peace that settled upon the town wasn't just the absence of conflict; it was the harmony born from a shared understanding, a bridge built not just with stone and mortar but with the language of Keshura, a language that whispered of respect, connection, and a future bathed in the light of a renewed covenant with all that existed. This was not just a return to the past but an evolution. The wisdom of the forgotten language was not a rigid set of rules but a dynamic philosophy that adapted to their changing world. As their society advanced, so did their understanding of Keshura. Years passed, and Enoch, his hair now streaked with silver, sat beneath the shade of a sprawling tree. Amara sat beside him, her face etched with the wisdom of time. The town had transformed into a vibrant city, a testament to the enduring power of the forgotten language. Flying machines dotted the sky, their movements echoing the patterns of constellations. Enoch looked around, a sense of deep satisfaction washing over him. He hadn't brought peace simply by teaching them the forgotten language; he had shown them how it could be a compass, guiding them towards a future built on harmony and respect. Keshura wasn't a relic of the past; it was the foundation of their future, a bridge that stretched not just across land and sky but across generations, ensuring that the song of Keshura continued to resonate for years to come. The aroma of roasting meats and sweet pastries hung heavy in the air, mingling with the vibrant chatter of a city transformed. Banners adorned with forgotten language symbols fluttered in the breeze, their once-cryptic symbols now a source of pride and understanding. Today, the city celebrated Enoch, the bridge walker, who led them back to the forgotten language, Keshura. A platform, meticulously carved with heavenly patterns gleaned from the forgotten language, stood at the heart of the bustling marketplace. Upon it, Enoch, his weathered face etched with humility, stood beside Amara, their hands clasped in a silent testament to their shared journey. The crowd's cheers rose like a tidal wave, a sound that resonated with a newfound unity. It wasn't the forced, hollow cheers of past celebrations but a joyful eruption of appreciation for the man who had shown them a path towards a brighter future. Children's faces painted with vibrant symbols mirrored heavenly constellations led the festivities. Their dance, a rhythmic reflection of the forgotten rituals that had once been relegated to dusty scrolls, brought a smile to Enoch's lips. This celebration wasn't about him; it was a celebration of the future they were building together, where the wisdom of the forgotten language wasn't just knowledge but an intrinsic part of their lives. A young woman, Elara, her eyes sparkling with admiration, stepped forward. She embodied how Keshura had breathed new life into their society. Her flying machine, a marvel of engineering interwoven with heavenly principles gleaned from the forgotten language, hovered proudly above the crowd. It wasn't a horror of metal and smoke but a graceful creation that moved with the elegant efficiency of a bird in flight. "Enoch," she declared, her voice ringing across the square, "you opened our eyes to the forgotten language, not as a relic of a bygone era but as a compass. You showed us how to live in harmony with the land, the stars, and each other. You didn't just teach us forgotten words. You taught us a forgotten way of life." Thunderous applause erupted, echoing off the surrounding buildings. Musicians, their instruments crafted with an understanding of the earth's natural frequencies, filled the air with a melody that resonated with the soul. It wasn't the discordant music of the past, where instruments competed for dominance; it was a symphony born from their connection to the world around them, each note complementing the other, creating a harmonious tapestry of sound. Artisans, their skills honed by a newfound appreciation for the earth's resources, presented Enoch with a magnificent sculpture. It wasn't just a lump of stone carved into a likeness but a representation of the bridge he had walked – a bridge between humanity, the land, and the divine. Crafted from local stone and adorned with shimmering metals mined with respect for the earth, it symbolised the strength and resilience in understanding Keshura. Enoch, overwhelmed with gratitude and a hint of disbelief, addressed the crowd. His voice, raspy but filled with sincerity, spoke of the power of community, of learning from the past, not to dwell on its mistakes, but to use its wisdom to build a better future. He didn't claim credit for their progress; he acknowledged their collective journey, their shared commitment to a life guided by the forgotten language. He spoke of the visions, the challenges, and the triumphs, weaving a narrative that resonated with everyone present. As the sun dipped below the horizon, casting a celestial glow upon the city, a bonfire roared to life, its flames licking at the twilight sky. Young and older people gathered around it, sharing stories of their day, their ancestors, their connection to the land, and their hopes for the future. The forgotten language wasn't just spoken in hushed tones during rituals; it was woven into the fabric of their conversations, a constant reminder of their chosen path. It was how they treated each other with newfound respect, nurtured their land with a deeper understanding, and looked up at the stars with a reverence that transcended mere curiosity. This wasn't just a celebration of Enoch; it was a celebration of a reborn city. It was a testament to the enduring power of the forgotten language. This bridge united them as a society and a community living in harmony with the universe. And under the watchful gaze of the stars, the city pulsed with newfound energy, a promise of a future bathed in the light of Keshura, a future they would build together, one forgotten word, one harmonious note, one act of respect at a time. The celebration would fade, the food would be devoured, and the fire would eventually die down, but the lessons learned, the connections forged, and the spirit of Keshura – would echo through the city for generations. The city's celebration of Enoch and the forgotten language, Keshura, stretched beyond the joyous festivities of the day. A ripple effect, subtle yet profound, began to reshape their society. Schools incorporated the forgotten language into their curriculum, not just as a collection of words but as a philosophy woven into every subject. Math's lessons explored heavenly patterns, history classes delved into the forgotten civilization's respect for the environment, and art classes echoed the natural world's colours and textures. It wasn't a mere rote memorization; it was about fostering an understanding of the interconnectedness of all things. Children, their minds unburdened by preconceptions, embraced this new way of learning. During astronomy lessons, they sang forgotten songs about constellations and built miniature houses using sustainable materials in architecture classes. They painted murals depicting scenes from forgotten myths on the city walls. The forgotten language became more than words on a page; it seeped into their daily lives. Farmers, armed with forgotten agricultural practices gleaned from Keshura, nurtured healthier, more sustainable crops. Inspired by the forgotten language's emphasis on balance and harmony, architects designed buildings that complemented the natural landscape. Fueled by Elara's pioneering example, engineers focused on developing clean energy sources and sustainable technologies. This wasn't just innovation for the sake of progress; it was innovation imbued with the spirit of Keshura. The city itself began to transform. Parks, once neglected patches of green, bloomed with diverse plant life, attracting a vibrant ecosystem of birds and insects. Skyscrapers, previously imposing glass and steel monoliths, were retrofitted with green roofs and gardens, transforming the once-sterile skyline into a tapestry of urban oasis. The forgotten language fostered a sense of responsibility towards the environment. People no longer saw nature as a resource to be exploited but as a partner to be respected. Recycling programs became second nature, waste minimization became a badge of honour, and public transportation, powered by clean energy sources, became the preferred mode of travel. News of the city's remarkable transformation spread everywhere.

Delegations from neighbouring settlements arrived, eager to learn from their success. Enoch, no longer just a bridge walker, became a beacon of hope, an inspiration for others seeking a path toward a sustainable and harmonious future. He shared his experiences – the visions, the challenges, and the triumphs - with these visitors, not as a blueprint to be followed blindly but as a spark to ignite their journeys toward a better future. Once lost to the sands of time, the forgotten language had been rediscovered not as a dusty relic but as a vibrant philosophy. It wasn't a rigid set of rules but a dynamic guide, reminding humanity of its place in the grand tapestry of existence. And as the city pulsed with life, bathed in the light of a sustainable future, the forgotten language continued to resonate, a constant whisper on the wind, a promise of a world where humanity and the universe thrived in a symphony of harmony. A shadow fell across the table on Enoch's porch, momentarily breaking the couple's quiet breakfast routine. Elara stood before them, no longer the wide-eyed dreamer who had enthralled them with visions of flight. Now a council member, her youthful face was etched with a seriousness that belied her years. "Enoch, Amara," she began, her voice hesitant, "something is troubling me." Enoch gestured for her to sit, the familiar warmth of concern blooming in his chest. Over the years, Elara had become like a daughter to them, her brilliance and unwavering spirit a constant source of pride. To see her brow furrowed with such a weighty concern gnawed at him. "What is it, Elara?" She took a deep breath. "News has reached us from a neighbouring city. They speak of a new God, a powerful entity who promises prosperity and protection." A flicker of unease crossed Amara's eyes. Enoch, but remained stoic. He had borne witness to the seductive whispers of false idols in the visions from the pool. The forgotten language, Keshura, was not just a way of life but a bridge to the one true divine, the Holy One, whose presence echoed in the heavenly dance of the stars and the rustling whispers of leaves. "And what troubles you about this?" he inquired, his voice gentle yet firm. "Some in the council," Elara continued, "believe we should consider this new God. They are swayed by the promises of wealth and safety, a future free from hardship." Enoch leaned back in his chair, the weight of his past swirling in his mind. He had seen the seductive allure of false prophets in the visions. Glittering cities devoid of spiritual connection, humanity is reduced to cogs in a machine, all in the pursuit of prosperity a jealous deity promises. The forgotten language, Keshura, was not just a collection of words but a shield against such deception. "Elara," he began, his voice laced with a wisdom honed by experience, "the path of the Holy One is not always one of ease and immediate riches. It is a path of balance, of understanding our place within the grand design, a harmonious dance between humanity, the land, and the divine." "But what if this new God offers a shortcut?" Elara pressed, a hint of desperation creeping into her voice. "What if it truly does bring prosperity without the struggle?" Amara reached out and placed a hand on Elara's. Her touch, as always, was a balm, a reminder of the deep connection that transcended generations. "The Holy One does not need to compete with empty promises," she said softly. "The harmony we've cultivated, the advancements we've made —all testaments to the blessings we've received by following Keshura." Enoch nodded in agreement. "The visions," he revealed, his voice grave, "showed me glimpses of a future where humanity strayed from the path. They worshipped false idols, seeking power and control, and it led to devastation." He recounted the vision of the sterile pods, a future devoid of human connection and spiritual fulfilment, a chilling reminder of the price humanity paid for chasing empty promises. Elara listened intently, her youthful face etched with a growing understanding that chased away the flicker of doubt. "The Holy One does not demand blind worship," Enoch continued. "Keshura teaches us to live in harmony with the land, each other, and the divine spark that resides within all things. It is this connection, this understanding of our place in the universe, that brings true prosperity that enriches the soul as much as it does the body." Elara rose, a newfound resolve in her eyes. "Thank you, Enoch, Amara. You have reminded me of the true foundation of our city's success. I will speak to the council. We will not be swayed by empty promises of prosperity built on shifting sands. We will continue to walk the path of Keshura, for it is the only path that leads to a future bathed in the light of the Holy One's grace." As Elara left, Enoch and Amara exchanged a silent look. The forgotten language, once a fading whisper on the wind, had become a shield against the allure of false prophets. The bridge they had built was not just between humanity and the land; it was a bridge to the Holy One, a constant reminder that true prosperity lay not in material wealth or fleeting promises but in living in harmony with the divine melody that resonated throughout the universe. In Elara's unwavering spirit, they saw not just the future of their city but the enduring legacy of Keshura, a testament to the enduring power of faith and the harmonious connection between humanity and the divine. Enoch sat on his porch gazing at the familiar dance of constellations when a profound stillness descended. The air crackled with an unseen energy, sending shivers down his spine. Sensing his unease, Amara placed a hand on his arm, her touch a grounding force amidst the swirling uncertainty. Then, the world dissolved around them with a blinding flash of light. Enoch found himself standing on a desolate plain, the once vibrant colours of his city replaced by a sickly grey. The air hung heavy with an acrid stench, and a chilling wind howled, carrying whispers of despair. Panic clawed at his throat. Where was he? What had become of his beloved city? A booming voice, echoing from the inky blackness above, shattered the silence. "Enoch, bridge walker," it resonated, devoid of warmth, "you have witnessed the consequences of straying from the path." Enoch squinted, searching for the source of the voice, a cold dread settling upon him. He recognized the desolate landscape –mirrored a fragment from one of his visions by the pool. In this future, humanity abandoned the forgotten language, Keshura, and the harmony it fostered. Celestial figures materialised before him, their faces obscured by shadows. They were not the benevolent beings he had glimpsed in his earlier visions but entities radiating a cold indifference. "The humans have forgotten," the voice boomed again. "They have polluted their land, worshipped false idols, and severed their connection to the divine." Enoch felt a surge of defiance rise within him. "But... Keshura," he stammered, "we brought them back to the path of the Holy One. We rebuilt our city based on its principles." The figures chuckled, a sound like wind whistling through a graveyard. "A noble effort, bridge walker," the voice echoed, "but ultimately futile. Corruption breeds within humanity, a festering wound that cannot be healed." Enoch's heart pounded with a growing sense of dread. Where was the hope, the promise of a better future he had strived for? The voice continued, "You, however, have proven your loyalty. You will remain here, a witness to the consequences they have wrought." Terror flooded Enoch's veins. To be separated from Amara, his city, and the life he had helped build felt like a punishment worse than death. "No!" he cried, his voice barely a whisper swallowed by the vast emptiness. "This is your reward," the voice declared, devoid of compassion. "To witness the inevitable fall of a civilization that refused to learn." Then, with another blinding flash of light, the desolate plain vanished. Enoch reappeared on his porch, the familiar scent of Amara's lavender oil filling his nostrils. But the world felt different, the weight of the vision pressing down upon him like a leaden cloak. Amara, her face etched with concern, rushed to his side. "Enoch! What happened? You were gone for just a moment, but you seem..." He choked back a sob, unable to tear his gaze away from the starlit sky. Once a source of comfort and guidance, the constellations now seemed to mock him with their indifferent twinkling. Was this the end? Was their journey, all their efforts, destined to crumble into dust? He turned to Amara, her face a beacon of hope in the encroaching darkness. He saw a reflection of his fear and a flicker of defiance in her eyes. They had faced challenges before, and they would face this one together. "Amara," he rasped, his voice thick with emotion, "I... I have a vision to share." He recounted the desolate landscape, the chilling voice, and the devastating prophecy. Amara listened intently, her hand clasped tightly in his. When he finished, a long silence stretched between them, broken only by the mournful cry of a distant owl. "This is not the end, Enoch," Amara finally said, her voice firm, her gaze unwavering. "This is a warning, a call to action. We will redouble our efforts. We will remind everyone, young and old, of the importance of

Keshura. We will build a future so strong, deeply rooted in the principles of the Holy One, that even the whispers of doom will not prevail." Enoch looked at her, a spark of hope reigniting within him. He may not know the future, but one thing was certain – he was not alone. Together, with Amara by his side and the unwavering spirit of their city, they would fight for the future they had envisioned, a future bathed in the light of Keshura. Humanity and the divine lived in harmony in this future, a future that defied even the bleakest prophecies.

Printed in Great Britain
by Amazon